Endorsements

"The tools and insights Mary Anne shares in her book are instrumental in polishing communication, presentation, and negotiation skills to achieve results. It's required reading for anyone striving to engage, build relationships, and improve outcomes to become more effective at work or at home. If you want to become more successful, this book provides practical examples and techniques to 'pull it all together' for success!"

—Shari Guess, Manager,
Sales and Corporate Staff Development
BenefitMall

"This book changed my business forever! By using *The Sales Messenger* in a book club format, I took my business from part time to full time, increased my self-confidence and currently sell services and products at a level I never imagined possible."

Carrie Cain, Founder,
Home Décor

"Mary Anne (Wihbey) Davis' *The Sales Messenger* is a must read for anyone who aspires to enhance their sales techniques and earning potential. Mary Anne takes us on a journey with struggling sales professionals and their mentor. The ten sessions take them to new heights of personal and professional success. Learning how to communicate effectively, with purpose and with your prospects best interests at heart is an art form that few can master. The new sales language skills, tips and communication styles presented, along with application of the lessons will help you accomplish this. *The Sales Messenger* will leave the reader with new insights on how to achieve your goals and dreams along with the added benefit that comes from mentoring others. The message delivered in this book will leave you entertained and a more polished sales professional so you can 'leave with your flags flying.'"

Elizabeth Henry, Vice President,
Consumer Sales and Service,
Docomo Pacific

"This book is as impactful today as it was when I first read it seven years ago. Only this time, I can fully grasp the simplicity and power of Mary Anne's insights. This 'sales' book is written as a novel, about a couple of individuals, just like you and me, trying to grow their businesses. Mary Anne teaches not all sales activity is created equal and your growth results happen as a result of being intentional with your time and efforts. Sales aren't just about the product, but how you communicate with the prospect. Read this book; study it; follow the steps and watch your money making activities become a reality!!"

Tracey C. Jones, President,
Tremendous Leadership

THE SALES
MESSENGER

THE SALES
MESSENGER

*10 Lessons for Sales Success
in Your Business and Personal Life*

MARY ANNE
(WIHBEY) DAVIS

THE SALES MESSENGER
*10 Lessons for Sales Success
in Your Business and Personal Life*

Published by:
Tremendous Leadership
P.O. Box 267
Boiling Springs, PA 17007

717-701-8159   800-233-2665

www.TremendousLeadership.com

ISBN: 978-1-94903-303-8

Printed in the United States of America

DEDICATION

This book is dedicated to Jor Molchan, of Weymouth, Massachusetts, whose ability to lead and convey these skills led all those committed to achieve extraordinary results. As a leading general agent, his coaching made a monumental difference in my life and was a powerful tool in my own personal success throughout the years. His passion for sales was the inspiration for this book and the foundation of the training I do today. May the lessons in this book guide you to a new level of success in your career and your life. He always said, "Leave with your flags flying."

TABLE OF CONTENTS

INTRODUCTION

As I'm rushing to get to my networking meeting I begin to wonder if this group is really worth my time. We meet weekly for the sole purpose of sharing leads, networking, and mentoring people who are new to our group. Just a year ago we had twenty members, and now we're down to six. We've had a few come and go, but for some reason, most of the people who came to the group didn't see the value of our "professional sales association." I'm starting to see why. We have become great friends, but none of us are really busting our quotas. We are in such different markets that we rarely share leads, so it seems like we spend a lot of time chatting, catching up, and even talking *about* our businesses. Meeting with this group is not impacting my bottom line; it's just a monthly activity that has been plugged into my calendar.

Everyone would be very hurt if I dropped out. What they don't realize is that I have several other networking meetings I'm involved in, as well as being a volunteer for Community Treasure, a local charity. It seems as though my life never slows down. Each day I have to get the kids off to school, take them to their activities, and take care of my personal and professional to-dos. It seems that countless things are eating my time. Ah, but they are great friends, so here I am for another breakfast. Here's a closer look at the group.

Bob Bailey, whom I have known for years, has been in sales for a long time with a variety of technology companies. He is now the sole salesman for See Me Now, a revolutionary videoconferencing methodology for personal and business use. Bob has been under a lot of pressure as the consumers are slow to adopt the product, while the company has him under the gun to make sales now. He has big-name competition, and I know that the few accounts that have purchased the product are not enough to put his product on the map. Bob is worried that if he does not hit a big one soon, he will be fired.

Patty Stillman was a corporate trainer for many years until she got laid off two years ago and joined a national training company as a contract trainer. When she signed on, she did not realize she would have to sell the training she delivers to corporate America. Aside from formal technology training, her company offers some self-study products that teach word processing, spreadsheets, and other software technologies. Patty receives a small draw against commissions, but her sales aren't high enough to sustain her. The last time we met she revealed that she might have to get a part-time job at the mall on nights and weekends just to keep the roof over her head.

Of course, others have the same story. Fred, who has his consulting business and charges a hefty fee for management and sales training, even admitted that without his wife's income, he would be back in the corporate world tomorrow. Betty is a travel incentive planner primarily selling cruises and vacation packages. She complains about getting beaten up by the airlines' special packages and online travel websites. Then there is Paula, who sells printing services. Actually, I think she seems to do OK, but like all of us, she has her moments. As for me, I have been selling insurance for several years. I make a good living, but with all the expenses, it seems, at times, that I am living hand to mouth. Together, our team provides a combination of stories and hard times, successes and failures.

As I approached the door of Sal's Diner, our regular haunt, I decided I was going to have to address my concerns to the group, and perhaps together we could find a way to make our time more productive.

We all said our pleasant hellos. Our regular waitress joined in on the greetings, too. Of course, after a year, she knew our typical order and asked, "The same today?"

Her question led me to my approach.

I replied, "No, today I would like a change. Let me have some eggs over easy, with some bacon and hash browns."

To my surprise, Bob chimed in and said, "That sounds good, I'll have that, too."

After everyone placed food orders, I said, "Gang, I changed for a reason. I have to be candid: I love you guys and I love the friendships we have created, *but* I am just so busy. My insurance business leads me to see clients day and night. The Community Treasure campaign has just begun so I am on appointments for them as well. I also have some other groups that I'm involved in, never mind trying to find time for family, friends, and fun. I just don't know if I can keep meeting for the sake of meeting. I'd like to know what we might do to make our time together more productive."

Immediately Bob chimed in and said, "I think we should make it mandatory to bring a certain number of leads to the table every week."

Patty objected. "No, that leads to too much pressure, and the leads might not be qualified leads."

Another asked, "How about we bring in speakers?"

All I could think of was that speakers would just be more *blah, blah, blah.*

So I said, "No, I think we get enough of that elsewhere. When we started meeting we believed it was our interaction that would make us different."

As our food arrived, Bob said, "Well, you know, I have been feeling the same way. I am the only sales rep in this region for our company, and what I miss are the Monday morning sales meetings. When I was with my last company we had a sales meeting every Monday to focus on our activity, results, pending and closed cases, and sales ideas. Back then, I always made or exceeded my quota and met my financial goals for my family. Sometimes I feel we are blaming everything, including the economy, when maybe *we've* never learned professional sales skills."

Right then I knew he had it. Our eyes were concentrating on him, with our hands on our chins, while nodding our heads in agreement. He went on to say he went to a one-day program recently and heard a man named George Melchan speak. This gentleman spoke not only on the strategic part of the sales or marketing plan but the tactical skills that help you know what to say, how to say it, and when to say it. As a matter of fact, after that seminar Bob had even looked at his website.

Bob said, "I am sure we can't afford him, but maybe he can recommend someone to coach us." We agreed to let Bob pursue this so we could discuss our options.

Later that afternoon, we were astounded at the offer George Melchan made to us. Bob emailed us and said George had agreed to coach us at no charge if we agreed to his terms:

- Commit to ten 90-minute Monday morning sales meetings. These meetings would begin promptly at 7:30 in his office.

- The sessions would be complimentary unless we missed a meeting or were late, in which case we would pay an amount equal to his time.

- Use the communication skills we learned in our personal and professional lives, in the written and spoken word.

- Do all homework assignments completely and on time.

- Commit to begin coaching and mentoring three other sales professionals having the same struggles immediately upon completing the sessions with George.

Based on the time constraints and penalty, only three of us (Bob, Patty, and I) decided to take him up on his offer.

Bob called Patty and me, placed us on a conference call, and together we phoned George to confirm. He set the start date, gave us a few assignments, and told us of some things he wanted to gather. We ended the call by thanking him for this generous offer.

George gave us a homework assignment before our first meeting, so I give you the same assignment before you read the first chapter. The rest of this book has an assignment at the end of each chapter so that you get the maximum benefit from the content. No one is watching you, so you're on the honor system. This book is about helping you be accountable and using the techniques that we learned many years ago, so that you can meet your goals, reduce stress, and most of all achieve your dreams.

Complete the assignment below before going to the next chapter.

Homework

1. Determine your financial needs and wants.

   - Figure out the income level you need to survive. Consider personal and business expenses, including networking meetings, advertising, education, and other expenses you might have.

   - Determine your goal—the amount of income that would make you say, "Wow, that was a great year!" Be sure it is realistic for a successful year.

2. List your top twenty-five prospects.

3. Determine the number of fresh prospects in your pipeline.

4. Find and/or print a summary of your company, including

   - Products and services offered

   - Current and desired markets

CHAPTER ONE

OVERVIEW

Know Where You're Going

If you don't know where you're going, you
may never get there.

—*Yogi Berra*

The three of us arrived at George's office promptly at 7:30 a.m. He led us into the conference room where he had coffee waiting. He was dressed professionally in an Armani suit. I noticed the monogram on his shirt cuff. I thought it odd that the monogram was CID rather than his initials.

George said that the fact that we took the time to call and request help was a great compliment to him. He set the tone for our sessions: "I hope that, at the end of the ten weeks, you will find a formal process of selling—from the approach to the close—and more important, that you will make more money and have more fun than you have had in years."

George then proceeded to set expectations. "We only have a short time together each week, and you will have to get used to my style. I will be frank and sometimes tell you things you don't want to hear. In ninety minutes, we don't have the luxury of beating around the bush, so I hope you will understand when I am direct in my approach. I have created two letters of expectations—what we can expect from each other and these meetings. Let's read them together, and if you are comfortable, sign it. Then we'll move on."

EXPECTATIONS AGREEMENT

What you can expect of me.

- You can expect me to begin the meetings promptly at 7:30 a.m. and let you out promptly at 9:00 a.m., so you may plan meetings accordingly.

- You can expect me to treat you professionally and candidly.

- You can expect me to teach you communication skills that you can use in all aspects of your life—as well as selling skills that will set you apart from the competition.

- You can expect that everything you tell me will remain confidential.

- You can expect me to have your assignments reviewed in advance, so we always make the best use of our time together.

Name: _____

Signature: _____

Date: _____

EXPECTATIONS AGREEMENT

What I expect of you.

- I expect you here and ready to work at 7:30 a.m. sharp.

- I expect you to complete all assignments and turn them in on time.

- I expect you to look at this venture as if you were starting a brand-new job today and to be open to the activities that will make you successful.

- I expect you to be here for all meetings unless you are physically unable to be here due to a major illness, contagious colds or the flu.

- I expect you to be open, honest, and candid about your situations.

- I expect you to keep confidential everything your peers say about their personal situation, companies, or products.

- I expect each of you to begin mentoring and coaching three individuals by the end of our time together, using everything you have been taught here including these expectations.

- I expect you to keep a positive attitude, and in your mind act like you are where you want to be.

I agree to these expectations. Should I not fulfill my assignments or attend a meeting, I can expect to be invoiced by George Melchan for his time.

Name: _____

Signature: _____

Date: _____

After everyone signed the agreement, we continued with the first session.

George said, "Selling is a great profession, and it troubles me when I see people with great potential who are struggling or whirlpooling around in a slump. Often it's because companies may not know what reps really need. Many sales managers today get promoted into management because they were great salespeople. They often may not know how to instill their skills in someone else, which is frustrating to both the manager and the sales rep."

George continued, "Now let me ask you a question. Would you agree that you can make more money in your role as a salesperson than in any other profession?"

We nodded our heads yes.

"Well, from your past experience, how much pure sales training do you get year to year? I am sure you receive training on your product and services. The question is, if selling is really your profession, what do you do to continually improve on your selling or communication skills?"

I replied, "When I was first hired years ago, we had a weeklong company school that focused mostly on selling. Since then, most company-sponsored training programs revolve around the product."

Bob stated that he had not been through a good sales course in over ten years.

George then said, "You see, everyone can talk theory of selling, such as 'It's all in relationship building' or 'You have to make a lot of calls,' and that is important. What separates the good from the great is that the great know what to say, how to say it, and when to say it in an honest, nonmanipulative, compelling, compliant manner—a manner that compels a person to take action with regard to your ideas, product, or services. We can all talk about the game of baseball and how it works, but the player must execute. In the Major Leagues, is spring training optional?"

"No," I replied.

George continued, "What would happen if the players did not go to spring training? Even the pros continually improve and practice the basics.

"Here's what I hope we accomplish in our sessions together." George turned his flip chart page to reveal this statement:

By the end of this time period, you will be able to deliver clear, compelling sales messages; have more qualified prospects than you have ever had before;

make more money; and most of all, do it without stress for you or your prospects.

"I will ask you to do things and sacrifice things in the next eight weeks that might be difficult. Everything that we will do will focus on your bottom-line results—key result areas and the acts that make you money."

George asked, "Based on your own experiences, what is the biggest challenge you are facing in your job today?"

I volunteered first. "I just seem pretty scattered, and I don't seem to accomplish what I need to, even though I'm working really hard. Selling insurance and financial products seems like a morning, noon, and night career. I am doing well, and I make the company convention every year. My income is OK, but not for as hard as I worked. Last year, I earned $70,000 in first-year commissions. Bonuses and renewals made my total income slightly over $100,000, but I have so many expenses, such as car, fuel, networking, meals, and entertainment. So, in my company's eyes, I am a top producer, but in my eyes, and my husband's eyes, we are living hand to mouth, even with his salary."

Bob spoke his turn. "Well, I feel the same way, but my biggest challenge is getting in front of people.

We have this great product. I am not sure, George, if you've heard of See Me Now, but I just can't seem to get in front of the right people. I make a ton of calls every day, and I am just not getting the results."

Finally, Patty said, "I have to confess, I'm just running out of money. My challenge is generating enough income from my training sessions and selling some of our other products to keep the roof over my head. I am ready to get a part-time job. I'm getting some prospective clients, but it is still not enough."

He listened carefully, never interrupting.

"Alright," he said, "let me clarify. I think what I hear you all saying is that you are working hard, gaining some momentum, but you are not seeing the results of your efforts. Is that correct?"

We all replied, "Yes."

"So, how do you balance your time to get the maximum results for your efforts? The first thing we need to do is really get a handle on where and how you are spending your time versus the income you need to survive. Then we will work on the superior goal, the amount you need to achieve your dreams. What I will say—especially to you, Patty—is don't ever quit when you are at the bottom."

He then said, "Always leave with your flags flying."

Plan Your Work, Work Your Plan

George used a baseball analogy to help us see how our own sales batting average would help us plan our goals.

"Every baseball player keeps statistics. Do you know yours?" He didn't wait for our answer. "First, we must determine how many sales you will need in order to reach your goals. Until we track your dialing and calling ratio, please make as many calls as possible."

George handed out a really nice calendar and said, "I would like you to start using this calendar. It may be similar to something you might already use. The main difference is that this one allows you to document your daily activity."

Giving these calendars was generous of George. He also gave us some colored highlighters. I wondered why I would need these things. They seemed antiquated compared to my iPhone.

He continued, "Many people do not realize there is a science to selling. Your numbers will reveal all."

We reviewed the calendar layout as he explained how to track information.

Dials	Contacts	Scheduled Appointment	Appointment Completed	Fact-Finding Appointment	Closed

"Note that there are places for you keep track of activity, which will be mandatory starting today. I want you to keep track of every dial, every contact, every scheduled appointment, and every kept appointment. Then keep track of the number of your fact-finding appointments, how many you closed, and how many agreed to buy your product or service. You can tally this information and then record the tallies in the back of the book where you can chart your weekly progress. This is not just another form to fill out. This information is vital for me to see how to improve your sales process. For example, Patty, if you tell me you are making fifteen to twenty contacts a week and only scheduling one, I know there might be a problem with your phone script."

Addressing me, he said, "Julie, if you tell me that you're scheduling fifteen people a week and only two are showing up for the appointments, this allows me to know that something in your voice may not be conveying the importance of your message or your time.

"Bob, if you tell me you asked eight people to buy your product and only one did, it might mean that you are not showing them how your product is a solution for their needs.

"Let's start with you, Patty. Looking at your goal sheet, I see that you need to earn $60,000 to keep the roof over your head and effectively run your business. Is this correct?"

Patty nodded in agreement.

"Patty, we have two months to turn you around. Based on the numbers you shared with me, you need 5K per month or about $1,250 per week." George then asked, "Now, how much is your average commission for your training seminars?"

"I get $500 per day for delivering a training session."

"Let's look at this picture more closely," George continued. "In order to meet your goals, you must have on your calendar two to three days of training per week. Now we just figure out how we get you there.

George turned to me and said, "Julie, if you want an income of $120,000 in commissions, which is your superior goal, you need $10,000 per month. Let's say your average commission is $1,250. You need to be closing two sales per week, or $2,500 in commissions. Later we'll work on figuring out, based on your calling ratio, how many calls you have to make to achieve this."

George continued showing us how we would use this calendar. "Turn your attention to the back of the calendar, where you can see the entire year on one page. Now you'll color code your time. We must be sure you are using your time wisely."

He flipped the page on his flip chart, and there he had written:

GREEN	Key result areas: Activities that lead to income today, such as calls, prospecting activities, sales appointments.
RED	Administrative: Filing, proposals, admin, service calls, database entries.
BLUE	Time off: Vacation, personal, and family time.
ORANGE	Time off: Vacation, personal, and family time.

"For the next ninety days, I want you to focus solely on the green time, the things that make you money. Later, we will make sure you balance your personal, administration, and long-term planning time. Focusing on green activities that make you money might mean sacrificing some things that are already planned. This is the only way to get control of your schedule and your income. Otherwise, your schedule will control you, and you won't make the income you deserve."

George continued, "Now, it sounds like with all of you, your finances are tight. I firmly believe that you have to spend money to make money. In your opinion, do you believe you are worth more than $10 per hour?"

We all said, "Yes."

"Then I suggest that you get in the habit of paying people for the $10-per-hour stuff. This will free you to spend time earning what you're really worth. Now, if you cannot afford to pay someone at the moment, I suggest that you do the $10 stuff in your downtime, at nighttime or Saturdays. You can't let this admin stuff interfere with your moneymaking activities. For the next ninety days, I want you to focus your efforts on the things that contribute to your bottom line. In other words, you must be very focused on calling, interviewing, or delivering your product or services. Do you see these initials on my shirt? I live by this motto: Call, Interview, Deliver, or C-I-D. Each day you must work on these three things."

George made great sense, except I knew already that my first quarter would be a challenge. I then explained my situation. I gave him the following reasons for my dilemma.

- The first week of January it's hard to get in touch with prospects.

- My family comes to visit that first week in January.

- The company convention is the last week in February.

- We take the kids skiing during the February holiday.

George looked at me very seriously and said, "Do you want to do things the same old way, or are you ready to make some new leaps in your career?

I said, "Yes, but I have earned this convention, and the kids count on their trip each year."

"You may not agree with what I tell you, but if you want true success, you need to make some changes. Think of your career like a brand-new job. Would a new boss let you take off three weeks in the first quarter?

"Julie, look at this schedule," and he pointed to the first quarter. "This is prime green time for you. I agree, reaching your prospects the first week of January is hard, but right when you are ready to get your momentum up, you take a week off for the convention. I am sure it will motivate you, but does it add to your bottom line right now? Same with the vacation: one or both of these must go for this year until you get to a level where you can afford to take this time off."

I agreed. It was obvious I had to make some serious changes to get where I wanted to be.

George wrapped up the session by saying, "Before we part today, I would like your opinion on what we accomplished in this session."

I admitted, "It's really an eye-opener to see how little time I devote to pure selling."

Patty added, "It's just a real revelation for me. I was going through the day without any sort of plan and letting my to-dos and appointments control me versus me controlling them."

George reminded us that we *must* focus on green activities over the coming ninety days. He wrapped up the session by handing out a typewritten sheet with our homework assignment on it.

Homework

1. Keep track of all prospecting and sales activities, and evaluate your numbers at the end of each week.

2. Reevaluate your goals.

3. Identify how much time you spend on pure spelling activities and begin to color code your calendar, highlighting how much actual time is really spent in the green zone.

4. Bring any sales scripts or phone scripts to the next session. In your case, have them available to edit as you read the next chapter.

CHAPTER TWO

THE SALES PROCESS

Why is it the ship beats the waves when the
waves are so many? Because the ship has a
purpose.

—Winston Churchill

George started out by stating, "The purpose of today's session is to lay out the sales process in a seamless fashion. What this means to you is that every step of the sale will connect and you will have confidence in knowing when it is time to move to the next natural part of the sale. As we move forward, I will introduce you to bridge or transition statements that seamlessly take you from one step of the sale to another. Transition statements have two other purposes: they help you say the right thing most of the time and they also keep you in control, but not obvious control. Success in selling is knowing your prospect and planning your call strategy. We will also learn how to qualify prospects.

"Before we begin, let's define 'selling.' As I describe it, selling is an ability to persuade or convince people to your way of thinking as it relates to your ideas, your products, and your services. If you think about it, 80 percent of daily communications is selling. It is an ability to influence even in everyday communications. Everyone sells!" he exclaimed.

George then said, "Next, let's discuss the steps to the sale. What's the first step?"

I replied, "To get an appointment."

George said, "Is that the first thing you have to do, or is that a sale within the selling process? In other words, don't you have to sell someone on the idea of meeting with you? So if you are selling even an appointment, what is the very first step?"

Bob replied, "You have to sell yourself?"

George asked, "If you are selling yourself in the first step, how focused are you on the customer? We want to separate you from the competition, and I bet there are a lot of people selling themselves, but if prospects' ears are not open, how do these salespeople sound?

We replied, "*Blah, blah, blah.*"

"So in the sales cycle, I will ask again, what is the first thing you must do?" quizzed George.

I replied, "You have to get them into conversation, I guess."

"Yes," George agreed, "the first step, you must make a Connection. It could be a conversation, a startling statement that grabs their attention, but it's something that gets you to engage with them. You might often hear this referred to as the rapport step. It's about getting the prospect actively involved in the conversation so he or she is captivated, not held captive. If you are selling too early, as many people do, especially in networking settings, you are boring the heck out of people as they plot their escape from you."

George proceeded to say, "I refer to the second step as Create Interest. In other words, it's important to be interesting while we capture their interests, especially their needs, wants, and dominant buying motives. Too often people confuse this interest stage with fact finding and assume people are interested, so they go in with probing questions too early. If people are not interested or really ready to answer questions, they will shut down."

Then George asked, "OK, what is the third step?"

"The presentation," I said.

"Yes, you are partly correct," he said. "It's not about a presentation. Anyone can deliver a presentation. To be successful in selling, you must be able to deliver a Compelling Presentation. One that will motivate them to take action on your product, idea or service. or selling stage. In other words, here is your opportunity to show them the value of your product and service, and more important, what it can do for them."

George said, "What's the fourth step, and here's a hint, it is not the close."

Patty said, "I guess answering objections?"

George said, "No."

We were stumped.

"Patty, you bring up a good point. Often, a sales rep will wait too long to solicit questions, thus finding these questions at the time of the close in the form of an outright objection. You should be trying to answer objections during the presentation, so when you get to the close and you are asking them for a decision, they are ready to buy.

"The fourth stage is the Conclusion. After you deliver a presentation, no matter how compelling it is, often times, you have given the prospect a lot to think about. If you want to eliminate the "I want to think about" objection, or "Let me get back to you," you simply wrap up your presentation with a conclusion about what they said they wanted and how this program can do it for them. The better job you do in Step 2, the more relevant your Conclusion will be.

"The fifth and last step is the Close. The close should be the last part, and, if done correctly, should be the easiest part of the sale."

George then transitioned and stated, "Now, we can have the greatest salesperson in the world, but if he or she does not have qualified prospects, then being skilled is useless. Part of sales success is making sure you have the right people in front of you. I have known many salespeople who are proud of getting appointments, only to find the person sitting on the other side is not qualified. Wouldn't you agree it is important to qualify people before moving fast forward through the sales cycle? So, let's now talk about qualifying prospects. What are some things you need to know before you ask them to buy?"

I said, "Well, you have to know if they even need your product." George wrote on the flip chart the word "Need."

Bob then said, "You have to know if they have the money," and George wrote "Have a budget."

Patty said, "You have to know if the person is the decision maker." George wrote "Decision maker."

I said, "I have to know, for insurance purposes, if they have any medical problems." He wrote, "Insurability."

Then he listed two others. "You also should know not only if they *need* your product, but whether they *want* it," and he wrote "Want."

"Julie, most people need insurance. Is that right?"

"Yes."

"But how often do they call you because they want to buy a policy?"

"Never."

George said, "They may know that they need to save money. Yet how many people live hand to mouth? Need and want may not be the same thing. I may *need* a new roof on my home, but I may not *want* one."

Finally, George wrote the word "Motive" on the flip chart and asked, "How would you define 'motive'?"

Patty said, "It's a reason for doing something."

George replied, "Webster's dictionary describes it as 'an emotional impulse causing someone to act.' What was the last thing you bought on an impulse?"

Bob said, "I actually bought a new flat-screen HD TV last week."

George interjected, "Did your wife think you were acting reasonably?"

"I talked her into the logic."

He then said our last qualifier is knowing the prospects' dominant buying motive—that is, that number-one impulse that will cause prospects to buy from us today.

George smiled, "Sometimes we find ways to justify our emotional impulses and sell ourselves, or often we go the other way and have buyer's remorse. How often have you made a sale or thought you really had a hot prospect, when later the prospect did not want it, changed his mind, or suddenly showed a lack of interest?"

I said, "Well, that happens to me on occasion. It is like the prospect waits until he or she knows I am not in the office, and then leaves a message canceling the policy they just bought."

George said, "That's because they acted on emotion and maybe did not have the logic to back it up. People can make decisions based on emotion but really need the reasoning behind it to make it stick. I wonder how often, in this economy, upscale department stores are experiencing returns? Bob, can you remember what you were you thinking right before you bought your new TV?"

"Well," Bob replied, "we are having our annual Super Bowl party, and this year my family is even coming in from out of town. I just felt we needed a better TV."

George replied, "Tell me what you were seeing."

Bob said, "I guess I saw everyone *relaxing* versus *huddled* around our thirty-inch TV."

"Now," George said, "don't think I am strange, but put yourself at your own Super Bowl party. What do you taste?"

Bob said while laughing, "Iced tea and some chili."

We all laughed, too, and George said, "Yes, you see, usually when people are emotional, they are experiencing one of the five senses. Someone can talk about a diet for ten years and never lose a pound. Three months before a class reunion, they will drop what is needed and then some." He then asked us to list the motives of our prospects. "Do you know what might cause your prospects to act now? What might motivate them to do business with you? It's different for everyone."

After the exercise, he stated, "Too often, we don't do a good job of qualifying, and we assume we know customers' needs, wants, and motives. We explain how great our product is for what we think our prospects need and want. Our prospects react by saying, 'Oh, this looks great, I will think it over,' 'I have to check with so-and-so,' 'I am happy with what I have,' 'I will get back to you later,' etc. They do this because you did not do a good job of qualifying and selling to their particular needs, wants, and motives.

"When you qualify your prospects, whether on the telephone or in person, the art of questioning is very important. I would like you to insert this next bridge or statement when you find yourself transitioning to questions. It might sound like this:

THE BRIDGE
"My purpose at this time is to get your answers to a few questions. Do you mind if I ask them?"

"Then proceed with your questions. Be careful not to interrogate them. Always get permission to ask questions. Otherwise they will feel interrogated and may possibly shut down. Or you might transition with, 'To make the best use of our time when we are together...'"

As we concluded, George said, "As a homework assignment, I would like you to write down what questions you use to qualify prospects either on the phone or in person. Next week we will work on how to really get customers excited to talk to you before you have ever told them a thing. I would also like for you to think of your ideal prospects and what might be their underlying motives that would cause them to do business with you. For example, Patty, if you are calling on the human resources department, the motives might be recognition or reduced turnover… which means less paperwork, fewer exit interviews. Remember to continue to monitor your activity so we can see if these new scripts are working. When we meet next week, our goal will be to improve upon your daily conversational skills to get people interested before you formally ask for an appointment.

"Before we part today, what's the one most important thing you learned in this session today?"

I jumped in and said, "It's really important to put yourself in the customer's shoes and to identify problems and solutions for each specific person."

Bob said, "Well, for me, it was learning to focus on getting the appointment. I knew it in theory, but I probably talk about the product far too much on the phone."

Patty humbly said, "For me, it was qualifying the prospect. I will talk to anybody who will listen, when in fact most are not even the decision makers or even a prospect. I just thought because they were from the company I wanted to target, that was close enough."

She continued, "So, in order to keep the prospect in the sales process and to present your product or service in terms of the benefit to this particular prospect's situation, I also learned that you have to start with some questions."

George thanked us for our participation and commitment. We all departed feeling a little more confident, a little closer to our goal of being professional salespeople who stand above the crowd.

Homework

Here's the assignment George gave us at the end of the session for week two. As always, to make the most of your time reading this book, do this assignment before going on to the next chapter.

1. Write down the questions you use to qualify prospects either on the phone or in person.

2. Identify your ideal prospect; list the underlying motives that would cause that prospect to do business with you.

CHAPTER THREE

THE ART OF ENGAGEMENT

Marketing and Your Messaging

The most important things are hardest to say, because words diminish them.

—*Stephen King*

I arrived promptly at 7:10 a.m. Sure enough, George was already waiting with coffee brewed. The other two followed shortly after. We fixed our coffee and made some small talk. George was a charismatic man, rugged yet polished. He wore the lines on his face with pride. I still could not believe he was doing this for us without a charge.

At 7:30 on the dot George transitioned to the business at hand by saying, "Let's get started. Today, I hope to help you make the best use of your green time by filling it with more qualified prospects. You'll do this by making your messaging more interesting, so that prospects are excited to meet with you. In short, we want to separate you from the competition and have prospects lined up for your services.

"Last week, I promised that I would help you get prospects interested before you ever asked them for a meeting. Before we get started, I want to review your activity and talk to you a little about your networking efforts. Let's review your numbers to see how your scripts worked and what we can do to get you in front of more prospects."

Surprisingly enough, we found Patty and I had more appointments. Patty had called on one of George's clients, a large healthcare company. She closed a three-day training seminar for the company's call center. She also shared that she is in Toastmasters and is terrified because, in the next few weeks, it is her turn to give a presentation on what she does. She knows that many in this group are her prospects. George assured her that the skills we are using can be used in both the written word and the spoken word, and can be easily applied to public speaking and training sessions.

George was thrilled when I told him I had four appointments with business prospects this week. Two of them were current clients that own small businesses. Bob had improved results, too, although he was still struggling with getting appointments. George asked Bob, "You said you are making a lot of calls. How many did you make last week?"

Bob replied, "I made thirty-four dials, reached eight, and did not get any appointments." He explained, "I can get them on the phone, but they just seem to put me off to the technology departments. When I get technology, they say they are not interested, and they talk about the budget, etc."

George said, "Perhaps you need to consider getting specific names of individuals you need to speak to before you start the calling process. I do not believe in cold calling for the sake of calling. It is not only about the sheer volume of calls you make, but it is more about the effectiveness of each call. Cold calling can sometimes be the least productive way of trying to get a sale. That's because people do business with those whom they like and trust. And if you are making a lot of cold calls, people are not as likely to trust you because they do not have a point of familiarity or reference. Your chances for sales success are dramatically increased if you first try to establish a point of reference with the prospect. This is why getting referrals can be very effective. In other words, if you can say to the prospect something like 'Your colleague Pat

Richards felt that you would really benefit by taking a few moments to meet with me to learn how I can help double your business,' you will have a much better chance of getting an appointment and ultimately closing the sale. We will talk more about the importance of referrals later."

George went on to say, "There could also be something in your script that is causing them to pass you off to technology. I am assuming you are saying something technical in your script, and you are not hitting on their problems, pain, or solutions."

Bob adamantly and earnestly replied, "I don't think so. I have worked hard at focusing on the solution, because I know that is important."

"Bob," George said, "let's role play. I will turn my head, because you can't have eye contact on the telephone, and listen to exactly what you are saying on the call."

George turned his back on us, became very serious, and said, "*Brinnng, brinnng...* Hello, this is George Melchan."

"Hello, George, this is Bob Bailey. I am with a new company called See Me Now, and we offer the latest tech—" Bob stopped and blushed as he heard where he was going.

George turned around, smiled, and said, "There. Now we can fix it! The client hears the name of your product and the word 'technology' in the first twenty words. Even if you go on to convey the solution, the person on the other end of the phone has formed a bias and sent you off to never-never land—the technology department."

"I can't believe I have been doing that for so long," Bob said.

George continued, "I asked you to make a list of your hot prospects, past customers, and target prospects. Let's focus on quickly getting in front of the right people, so we can make the best of your calling time. Bob, you mentioned that the economy is affecting your prospecting, and you said earlier that you can't seem to get in front of the right people, is this right?"

As he handed Bob a flyer George said, "Bob, look again at your flyer. In your opinion, is this something that makes a prospect who doesn't know much about your particular product jump out of his chair and say, 'I want to learn more'?"

Bob replied, "Well, no, I guess not."

George continued, "I agree. Any message, whether it's written or spoken, must be designed to capture someone's attention and interest.

"You say you are a new company in those early words. Well, today with all that has transpired, how many people want to do business with a new company? We will work on the art of messages later. Your early words are vital."

Next George asked us to look at our networking activities. He reminded us how we shared at the first meeting that our expenses were relatively high for networking compared to the results. All of us attend several networking meetings each month.

I attend two other networking clubs, and I attend two meetings per month for my industry. One of them is just for women. Bob is on the board of an association in his industry that is taking up a great deal of time, and Patty attends many luncheons, dinners, and networking meetings in the hope of generating some good leads. I shared with the group that only one group gave me a few leads. Generally, networking clubs have not been good sources, but I know that eventually people will give me some leads because of the relationships I have made. I shared that I love going to my industry meetings because I always get new sales ideas, and I am motivated by others who attend the meetings. My only problem is implementing some of the great ideas. The women's meeting was another that I felt compelled to attend. That group, like ours, tended to form as a group of friends. Occasionally we have a speaker, but rarely do we share leads as we all are in the same business. The group has dwindled, but the peer pressure would be great if I were to disappear. And of course, there is my volunteer work, which involves meetings for Community Treasure.

George asked us to consider being more focused in our networking meetings. He also reiterated the important point that people do business with those whom they like and trust.

He used me as the example. "Julie, you may make some great friends in these organizations, just as all of you do. The question becomes, why aren't you generating more productivity? The answer could be twofold. Maybe you have not been clear when you describe your services. As we saw with Bob, the minute he says the word 'technology' when he talks to people on the phone, they form a bias. So if you are starting off by saying, 'I am with XYX insurance company' before stating your commercial, prospects may be forming a bias. For example, they may associate you with the last TV commercial or experience they had with insurance. If they just had a fight over a car claim, they may associate you with property and casualty insurance when, in fact, I don't believe you are even licensed for those products. Are you?"

"I'm not," I said.

He said, "The other reason could be, which I find to be the case in many of these networking groups, that even though they may really like you, Julie, they may like and trust their own financial advisor or agent a little more. That means they may be referring what could be your prospects to their own personal agent or even a personal friend or family member. Just as I do not believe in calling for the sake of calling, I do not believe in networking for the sake of networking, or advertising for the sake of advertising. Networking not only costs you money, but it costs you your time, and all of you shared with me that time is scarce. I would like you to rethink your networking activities. If you are really gaining value, whether it's knowledge or leads, then keep going and get more active. If you're not, then I would ask you to back off from these groups, and let's get you active where your prospects are active."

George continued, "I will also share that good networking and relationships take time. If you are going to get involved where your prospects are, go because you want to go and contribute, knowing that in the long run there will be a return. There is nothing worse than a hyper vendor who comes into a specific group trying to sell all the members. You must contribute and show yourself as a valued resource to the group, and then and only then do you deserve the right to secure business from the group. Remember that in our first week we talked about the balance of your time. Are you spending enough time working on the areas that bring you results? Or are you keeping busy for the sake of being busy while not really being productive with your work activities?"

George continued to explain that he's a firm believer that all companies and sales reps should have a target market. Quoting the late Peter Drucker he added, "In the past, companies had mass markets and mass advertising. For example, in the 1970s there were cola wars. As Coke and Pepsi were battling, what product emerged out to compete?"

I replied, "Tab?"

He said, "No. Do you remember, 7-UP, the UnCola? Peter Drucker also stated, 'To survive and thrive in the twenty-first century even these large companies would have to focus on a market niche and then move closer to the market.' You see, it appears to me when you are talking about your networking or leads groups, you are doing just that—mass advertising to mass markets. I am going to challenge you to really identify who, in fact, can benefit from your ideas, products, or services. Then I will ask you to find out as much as you can about them, including where they go, where they network, and even what they read. You must do this in order to effectively network with them. As I said, you must contribute, really delve in, give your time, become a resource to the group, and then you will become someone the group can trust. You might advertise to your niche market by writing articles or offering to give free presentations about solutions that will really solve their problems. I would like for you to think of your target markets or your ideal markets, and I want you to find out what associations they might frequent. Go and check out those groups, and see if you like and can live with them, because I want you to volunteer and get involved. If you don't like the feel of the group or have poor chemistry, then there is no reason to spend your time there. Remember, I told you I want you to have less stress and more fun in your work.

"For example," he said, "Bob, you said that corporate trainers are a prospect. Are you involved in any training groups?"

Bob shook his head no.

"Then go ahead and find out more about the National Association of Trainers and Developers. I am a member, and I know they meet locally once a month. Go to their website and find out more, and maybe go and evaluate their next meeting.

"Now, list your target markets, and let's brainstorm about where those prospects might be."

Patty suggested, "HR professionals are a good source," and she added that she knew there was an association but did not know much about it.

Bob added, "I bet you might find some HR people at the training meeting. Why don't we check that one out together?"

We continued to work on this for a little while, and we agreed we would also do some further research and inquiry into any other groups we might have missed.

"Let's work on this," George said. "All of you, I want you to think of your ideal prospect. Write it down. For example, Bob, who is your ideal prospect?"

"Corporate executives, sales reps, and trainers of large companies," Bob answered.

George said, "Since each one of those groups have different needs, let's take them one at a time. If you're sending the same message to everyone, it will be hard to get through to any one group. This next exercise will help you create mini-messages for the networking, telephoning, and even your marketing." He continued, "For homework, I asked you to identify your ideal prospect and the underlying buying motives. As you think about these prospects, what problems do they face daily that you can solve? Really think about their pain and how your solution can remedy that pain."

George instructed us to make two columns on a piece of paper. We were to write "Pain/Problems" on the left and "Remedy (Solution)/Pleasure" on the right. Here's what we drew in our notes:

PAIN/PROBLEMS	REMEDY (SOLUTION)/PLEASURE

Bob," George asked, "what pain does a sales rep face as it relates to your product?"

"Travel. They are tired of the hassles of traveling. They've had their travel budgets cut, which affects prospecting and servicing customers. And when they travel, that means time away from their own families. Today, we find people want to spend more time with their families."

George asked, "And how is their business?"

Bob said, "They, too, are hearing the economy objection, and their business may be slow."

George then asked, "What remedy or solution do you bring to the table?"

"Well, we can get them face-to-face with their clients without ever leaving their PC."

George replied, "Well, that is the solution, and so what pleasure does that give them?"

Bob said, "They can still service clients face-to-face while saving on their travel budget, and with our state-of-the-art technology they will have the very newest innovations in telecommunications."

"There you go again getting technical. Tell me in English! Now, let's work on your telephone script. Later we can apply this technique to general conversation, networking, and even your flyers. If you can understand a person's problems and pain, and know your remedy and what pleasures it brings to the prospect, then you can sell just about anything."

George then asked, "When it comes to the telephone, what is your main objective, or what are you selling?"

I replied, "Yourself."

Patty said, "Your purpose is to sell your service."

And then Bob said, "To sell an appointment."

George said, "Bob, you get the prize of the day."

Bob laughed and said, "I cheated because I remember that from your workshop."

"Well," George continued, "it is to get an appointment, and you must stay focused on this. Your phone call should be just a couple of minutes long in total, and it must be compelling enough to make them want to see you.

"I will introduce you to another bridge. Remember, these are transitional statements that, if memorized, will cause you to say the right thing most of the time. In other words, you will take your eyes from the product and turn your ears toward the prospect. These transitions or bridges will gracefully get you through each step of the sale.

"Before the bridge, however, you want to always remember to establish credibility right away, with your tone, inflection, greeting, and if possible, by mentioning the name of a mutually respected colleague who referred you to the prospect. Here is the bridge we will use for capturing their interest:

THE PURPOSE OF MY CALL TODAY IS TO:
_____
_____
_____
[State your objective or purpose of the call.]

George picked on Bob to try out the skill first. He said, "Ready? OK, Bob, go for it!"

Bob said, "The purpose of my call is to ask you for an opportunity to demonstrate our new product, See Me—"

George stopped him and said, "Remember, the name of the product, company, or service goes last."

Bob started again, "The purpose of my call is to ask for an opportunity to demonstrate how our product can put you in front of more clients and prospects without the expense and hassles of travel. Our product is the latest in videoconferencing. And unlike traditional conferencing, it can be operated from your laptop, incurs no long-distance charges, and your clients will love it because they don't have to take time away from their office to meet with you."

We all looked in awe, and Bob just blushed. The funny thing is that I finally started to understand what it is Bob sells, and to think, he'd been talking to me about it for two years.

George said, "Let's do another example, and then we will work on your messaging for networking, the telephone, and, as some call it, elevator prospecting. Patty, who is your ideal prospect?"

She said, "Usually the directors and managers within an organization and occasionally the human resource department."

George said, "Let's do this exercise again," as he placed two column headings on the flip chart:

PAIN/PROBLEMS	REMEDY (SOLUTION)/PLEASURE

"Patty," he said, "let's look over here on the left. And by the way, the other two of you can chime in. As I may have mentioned, after this process, you will be able to use this to apply to any sale and any industry.

"Patty, what are your prospects' problems and their real pain if they don't use your solutions?"

"Well, if their people do not have basic technology skills, they are less efficient and less productive."

George continued, "And what happens to a team or an organization when people are less productive?"

Patty replied, "Competition can get ahead of them, less work gets done in a day, efforts are duplicated because untrained employees have to ask someone to create their PowerPoint presentation for them."

"Patty," he asked, "what pleasures do they get from your remedy?"

"Well," she said, "the HR department will have better-trained workers, so they are less frustrated and will have fewer problems per employee. And the manager will have a better orchestrated team as he gets better productivity per employee."

And then George asked, "Yes, Patty, and what is the real pleasure to that HR person or that employer if there is greater productivity and there are better teams?"

She replied, "In the long run, the company will produce more and spend less, and that makes it a happier and healthier company."

"Let's try your phone script," George said.

"Hello, this is Patty Stillman of Employee Soluti—"

George stopped her right there and said, "Remember, the name of your product, company, or service is at the end of your statement. For now, let's work on the statement. We can work on fitting it into your full phone script later. As I said, this statement can be used in your networking and even in your flyers. So after your basic intro, and remember if possible, emphasize your referral source, start with your bridge—the purpose."

Patty said, "Hello. The purpose of my call today is to share with you how you can improve your bottom line by improving your employees' productivity.

I would like to ask for a few minutes of your time to discuss employee development to see if our seminars might be a fit."

We all exclaimed, "Patty, that sounds great!"

George looked at me and said, "Julie, you mentioned in your original assignment that you have been having difficulty getting in front of your current clients, especially those who have bought personal insurance and who have a business and have business insurance needs. Is that correct?"

I nodded my head in agreement.

He continued, "As well as you can remember, let me hear the script you used."

I mentioned how I had called a client at work just yesterday. "He is the owner of a print shop and has about ten employees. I called him and said, 'Hi, Jim, I would like to come by and visit and share with you some ideas for you and your employees.'" As I was rambling, I could see the sparkle in George's eye.

He said, "Julie, would you agree that people are busy today?"

I nodded, wondering to myself what he noticed about what I said.

"That brings up a question: How many people have time during the workday to visit? Remember, your first twenty or so words are so important, especially on the phone."

Once again, we held onto his every word. He said, "Well, think of the word you are using in your script...'visit.' The prospect most likely will shut his ears because, today, no one has time for a visit. I will take it one step further. When I hear the word 'visit,' I think of all the time my parents would drag me to a relative's house while they visited, and I just had to sit there bored out of my mind! The word 'visit' alone may send shivers down your prospect's spine. So let's make it compelling based on their pain and your solution. Try it again. Start with the purpose."

"Hi, Jim, this is Julie. The purpose of my call is to ask for the opportunity to meet so I might show you how you can retain qualified employees, improve morale, and even possibly take a tax deduction for some of your own retirement and insurance benefits."

"There now," George asked, "is that a little better?"

We all had this puppy-dog look on our faces, and I humbly stated, "Yes, it is." As he flipped over a page on his flip chart he said, "Here we have a few telephone tips."

PHONE TIPS
• Keep small talk to a minimum.
• State the name of your referral source up front.
• Speak with confidence; a little faster and louder and a lot clearer.
• Smile; it can be heard.
• Warm up: Stretch your neck and shoulders.

"This takes me to a related topic: keeping your pipeline full with fresh prospects. How many of the calls in your hot prospect list are just callbacks?"

Bob answered, "Most of the time, I call two, three, and even four times."

I said, "I would say 75 percent of mine are people I call back. They seem interested, just busy. Others just needed time to think about it, so yes," I said, "I think about 75 percent of my calls are callbacks."

George said, "You may not like this, but I'm going to suggest that you call any prospects on your call list one more time, and if they don't bite, remove them from your current prospect list. This is a hard thing to do, but I guarantee you if the *oomph* is gone, then they are just being nice to you. When you are calling back, often the insecurity is coming out in your voice."

In his mimicking voice George said, "Didya make up your mind yet? ...Is there anything else I can get to you...?" Then he continued, "It goes without saying, but the more you narrow your sales attempts down to qualified prospects who truly need or desire your product or service, the greater your chances of sales success. As I have stated before, you've got to let the deadwood go and start building your call list with qualified new prospects."

I thought carefully about this. I wasn't sure if he could read the concern on my face. I said, "I have a ton of people I keep calling back, some for appointments, and others whom I have done a lot of work for. I can't just throw them away." I said, "George, I have to admit, you are making sense, but I am scared. I guarantee you if I get rid of all my callbacks, I will be lucky to have ten people to call."

He said, "That's good!"

I looked at him as if to say, *Are you crazy?*

He said, "Now you will be able to fill your pipeline and get your sales off to a fast start. Remember, I told you, this venture with me would be like starting over again, and you are!

"You are not using time wisely if you are just calling the callbacks. These people have made a decision, even if that decision is indifference toward your product. To really excel, you must get fresh, qualified leads and improve upon your presentation skills."

George continued, "When you know you have done your best, when you know that you delivered a great presentation, if you cannot close it, you need to let it go. If you've done a good job, satisfactorily answered the prospect's questions, then it's the prospect's loss and not ours, and time to move on." This started to put it into a new perspective for me.

"Now, let's use the same technique to create your networking messaging. Remember to state three potential benefits and state your name, your company name at the end. Let's have some fun: Julie, I want you to create one for Community Treasure. Bob, I want you to create one for the association where you serve on the board. And last, Patty, I want you to create one for my new business. You can have one to three benefits. The bridge that leads you onto the message is 'we are in the business of _____, _____, _____,' and then state your name and your company after some time."

With a little help from George, I came up with "We are in the business of delivering hope, protecting our community, and making a lasting impact." Patty said, "Well, George, if I worked for you I would be in advertising. We're in the business of dramatically improving the lives of sales professionals through practical training solutions that can cut your sales time in half and let you enjoy the 'game' of sales."

Homework

1. Review your current pipeline; be courageous and eliminate the deadwood.

2. Call your top fifteen clients and ask them for referrals.

3. Write a brief message prior to each new appointment.

4. Write a closing message for the end of a meeting to set the stage for next time.

CHAPTER FOUR

BUILDING THE RELATIONSHIP

What is uttered from the hearts alone will
win the others' hearts to your own.

—*Johann Wolfgang von Goethe*

"The first important step is the Connection and it's the most important" George stated, "because if you cannot get people to connect with you, no matter how good your product is, you will starve. I want you to think about all the ways that a sales rep might connect or into a conversation with a prospect, and then we will see which of these may apply to you."

Patty said, "Shouldn't you talk about a mutual interest?"

Then I jumped in and said, "Yes, it's important that we should find something in common."

George responded, "So far, I hear you saying you make small talk about a common or mutual interest. Anything else?"

Bob then sat up in his seat and said, "I was taught that you look around the room and find something to talk about like their family, or even compliment them."

George said, "I hope that by the end of this morning, I will give you techniques that separate you from the competition, and take you from being a visitor to a great conversationalist whom your prospects look forward to seeing." He continued, "Think about what you said.

"Imagine what it would be like to be that purchasing agent of a large company where vendors are calling all day. Here is how it sounds." He spoke in a mimicking tone and said, "'Cute kids, is that your wife, how about that football game last night?'

"Now imagine it's a rainy day. You say, 'How 'bout that weather out there?' The purchasing agent was probably depressed after being constantly reminded that it was nasty outside!

"The techniques we will work with are designed to separate you from the competition and more important, to help you build and maintain relationships to last a lifetime.

"Let's look at all the ways sales reps and vendors get into conversation and identify which techniques will work best for you. Are you ready? I will run through these, and I want you to think which may apply to you."

We nodded in agreement.

"First, you both mentioned common or mutual interests. It certainly is an effective way to get into conversation. The challenge sometimes can be to get out of the conversation step when you have that mutual interest. Remember, people in business today rarely have time to visit, or you take too much time. You must bridge from conversation to business in the appropriate amount of time—that is, just a few minutes. You might use a transition statement like: 'I know you are busy, and the purpose of my coming by today is...' The prospect may have had a great visit with you and even like you. The next time you call, the prospect may put you off because you took a lot of time. In the worst scenario, the prospect feels you took the time, even if the prospect did all of the talking.

"Second, I am surprised that none of you mentioned something about the person who referred you to the prospect. I hope you are working your referral sources and more importantly using the name in the early part of a conversation, whether it is a phone call or a letter. Do you use referrals?"

I replied, "Well, I get some. I have to admit that sometimes when I make a sale, I forget to ask."

Bob said, "I used to be better at them. I have a few, but I am making a lot of cold calls."

Patty said that because she is getting her business going, she needed some, too.

George said, "OK, we will find some time in one of our sessions to further address the subject of referrals. There is no better way for an introduction. Remember, people do business with those who they like and trust, so an endorsement goes a long way in building rapport. When you have referrals, as I said, be sure to state the name up front. For example, you might say or write, 'Our mutual friend and my client—state their name—suggested I introduce myself to you.' Or, 'I am calling at the suggestion of so-and-so.'

"Third, what about a free gift? They've been used throughout time to get into conversations. The Fuller Brush man used to use them when he worked door-to-door, banks have used them, and for you ladies, how about those cosmetic counters? I think they never realized how well in fact it would work for them. I noticed my wife won't buy anything unless it is time for the free gift. The sad part is she will go to a counter and ask if they have a free gift and the untrained sales rep, who now has a live prospect in conversation, will say 'no,' then proceed to tell her when to come back for the gift and let her walk away! Do you think she is so loyal to that store that she marks it in her calendar to go back? Of course not. She waits until she sees a free gift offer somewhere sooner and buys it there.

"Julie, I know my insurance agent once gave me a laminated picture of the map of the United States. He finally opened up my mind to comprehensive planning when he told me his work is like a road map. It helps you identify where you are, plot where you want to go, and chart the smoothest, fastest route to get you there. The agent said, it would be like your wanting to go to California: you might know that it is west, but you certainly would not get in your car without the map! So my point is, if you have a gift for conversation, try to find a way to transition to business."

I must admit, I slumped in my seat. I did not dare mention I have been giving gifts for years, never thinking to use them as an analogy. I wondered if George could read the look on my face.

Patty excitedly said, "Hey, I have these little stress balls. I bought them for my seminars, but I bet I could give these at networking meetings. They are really cool, and people love to use them.

George said, "That is a great idea. Put them out in advance. Do they have your name on them?

"No," she said.

He said, "I would splurge and get your name, logo, and number on them, so when people take them back to work, they see your name. And the good part is if you are handing them to the right prospects, it could lead to work—paid work!"

George continued, "The fourth way to get the prospect into the conversation is to use big names. This could be anything from an internal center of influence all the way to advertisers using sports figures in their ads. For you, it might be listing any big-name clients you might work with, with their permission, of course.

"The fifth technique for conversation is an important one. Bob, you mentioned complimenting. I know that was taught many years ago. As a matter of fact, I was taught that, too. The truth is, Bob, if it is not sincere, it can backfire on you. Think of that purchasing agent sitting in the office, vendors coming in one by one, some vendors even indulging them in a good lunch or even golf, and the agent continually hears the same flattery and small talk. How sincere does it come off?

Bob replied, "Well, not very."

"How does he feel?" George asked.

Bob said, "Well, like, 'What do you want out of me?'"

"Bob, if we were strangers in an elevator and I said, 'That is a great suit,' how would you feel?"

"I would feel good."

George continued, "You see, flattery can be good, but usually when there is nothing to be gained by it. In a sales situation, not only is it boring conversation, it can backfire. So with complimenting, be sure not to compliment the obvious. Everyone is doing that.

"They look at the trophies, photos, or even the suit. Do some homework and find out something about the person in advance. You can find out a lot about people by looking at their social websites or even searching their name or their company name in Google. Also with compliments, don't ever compliment something unless you are prepared to tell them why you like it. When you say 'Thank you,' in written or spoken form, always say why. I love these customer service centers: 'We appreciate your business.... Your hold time is twenty minutes.'"

He said, "Number six, another way to build rapport and get into conversation is to send a handwritten note. Think about it: how often do you get your own mail? How excited are you to run and get it every day and, more importantly, open it?"

"Not very," I said.

"Julie, if you see a handwritten letter or note card with a real stamp on it, what do you do?"

I smiled and said, "I rip it open."

"Yes, probably before you get in the door. How often do you send written sincere compliments, thank-you notes, or a note of introduction? Remember, you need to set yourself apart from the competition! How often do you send your customers a sincere thank-you note on their decision to do business with you? This simple effort can eliminate buyer's remorse. I often received a five-dollar gift card from a Realtor, and it prompted me to call her and thank her. How ingenious—she engaged me in 'conversation.'

"Do you take the time to pass on compliments to a boss regarding the administrative staff, or something good you heard about someone? Find the time to contact that person to let them know what you heard.

"You see, I believe we all have an internal bucket, and this bucket gets filled with a lot of crud during the day. Maybe someone cut us off on the road, or we had a fight with our spouse, and then we get to work and deal with some office problem that should not be ours.... Our bucket starts to fill, and perhaps we have nowhere to empty it. Today, a lot of people are walking around with their buckets full. I believe it only takes one *sincere* compliment to empty someone's whole bucket.

"And that brings up a question: How often do you sincerely compliment or thank your administrative support, your children, your spouse, or your night workers—those who clean your office? I wonder how often those workers get thanked or complimented. Imagine how clean your office might be when you leave them a note or a gift.

"Here's a challenge for you: Keep three pennies in your pocket or somewhere where they will be visible for you. Each time you pass a sincere compliment, move a penny to your other pocket. Do this for thirty days.

"Another way to connect with your prospect is with a good story. You will find that many public speakers use a funny or compelling story to capture your attention.

"Patty, think about it: You are worried about your upcoming speech. Maybe you can come up with a story as an icebreaker relating to technologies.

"And one final way to connect and build rapport is to engage people with the use of thought-provoking statements or questions. These could be in the form of a question based on pain or even an alarming statistic. Both are powerful. These are designed to get your prospects' attention and have them say, 'Tell me more!' Good advertisers use these techniques, and you can, too. One of my favorite ads for long-term care insurance said, 'Congratulations, you are the proud new parent of a beautiful new seventy-seven-year-old,' and in the middle was the cutest little old man I ever saw. Maybe it just hit me, since my wife and I are caring for her parents as well as my mom. I now own long-term care. I'm not sure if it was the ad or the agent, but I still remember the ad.

"You can also use the questions to qualify your prospect throughout the sales cycle and to capture the person's interest at the same time. You may use these techniques in general conversation, including at the soccer game, or at the start of a business or networking meeting. They can be used in the spoken word and in the written word to capture attention and interest in your flyers, advertisements, emails, and memos."

Homework

George taught us some great techniques to capture our prospects' interest and to get them thinking.

1. "Sincerity"—compliment three people per day for thirty days.

2. Send five handwritten notes per week.

3. Begin to ask for referrals.

4. Think about the gifts that might reflect my businesses.

5. Bring a list of questions you commonly ask your prospects.

CHAPTER FIVE

THE ART OF QUESTIONING

Getting the Facts, Wants, Needs

Successful people ask the right questions,
and as a result get better answers.

—*Anthony Robbins*

Here we are, it's another Monday, another great meeting with George. As he began he said, "The purpose of today's meeting is to share with you the art of questioning. In other words, how to get answers to the questions you need while creating interest and engagement.

"Before we get started," he said, "let's review our qualifiers again. Who can remember all six that we discussed? Those things we need to identify before we ask for the sale."

I said, "I think I can."

He said, "Go ahead. I will write them down on the flip chart."

"Do they need our product?"

"Yes," he said as he wrote it on the flip chart "Number 1: Need."

"Do they want our product?"

"Right again," he said as he wrote "Number 2: Want."

"In my case they need to be insurable. Do they make the decisions? Do they have the money?"

"You are forgetting one," he said.

"Oh, yes," I said. "What could be their motive for buying?"

"Good. Now have you ever taken a sales course that tells you to ask questions?"

"Yes," I answered. "they tell you to ask a lot of open-ended questions."

"That's right," George confirmed. "There are countless questions you will need the answers to, so it is important to get the answers to these and other relevant questions. The problem with open-ended questions, when someone hits you with too many questions, you might feel interrogated. Your prospects can feel the same way. Or they may not be ready to divulge information, so in turn they don't give you honest answers. Questions are important, and more important is your ability to listen. We discussed this bridge before:

BRIDGE THREE

To make the best use of our time when we are together, my purpose at this time is to get your answers to a few questions. Do you mind if I ask them?

"I asked you to write down the questions you ask to qualify your prospects, so let's review those. What are the questions that you ask in person or on the phone to see if they are even a prospect?"

Bob shared the following questions:

- What are you doing now with videoconferencing?

- Do you use videoconferencing now?

- Why don't you use videoconferencing?

Mine were:

- Do you currently own any life insurance?

- At what age do you plan to retire?

- Do you have any retirement accounts now? What types?

Patty had a few, too: "What are you doing regarding the training of employees? Do you give them formal training on typing, word processing, or spreadsheet software?"

George then asked us if we had ever made a presentation only to find out that the person we were talking to was not the decision maker.

We all agreed we had experienced this more than once.

We discussed how important it is to find out the prospects' needs, wants, and motives, as well as their decision-making authority and budgets. George noted that none of our questions were based on decision-making authority, budget, or even true wants or dominant buying motives.

George said, "This is common, as sometimes it is uncomfortable to ask people about these things. Yet if you don't ask, they will haunt you as objections later on in the process. That is why it is so important to ask the right questions, at the right time, and in the right way.

"The first thing to do whenever you know you will be asking fact-finding questions is to diffuse the prospect's defensiveness with the bridge we used for phone calls—that is, 'In order to make the best use of our time together, my purpose at this time is to get your answers to a few questions. Do you mind if I ask them?'

"Let's move on to types of questions. The first type of question we will refer to are reciprocity, or give-and-take questions. These questions keep the conversation moving. Using give-and-take questioning invites the prospects to give you their honest opinion and then give you the opportunity to speak. It's like ping-pong, or some might call it meaningful dialogue.

"Julie," he asked, "how does one keep a free-flowing dialogue moving in the right direction?"

"I guess just ask questions and hope they give you the truth."

George said, "Well, there are key words you can use to try to solicit information as well as keep the conversation moving. One way is to not worry about selling too soon. Amateur salespeople go into sell mode too quickly. Even at networking meetings, for example, they go into telling about their products and services way too fast. When that happens, not only do they sound *blah, blah, blah,* they may also appear pushy and aggressive. If you can ask questions and acknowledge their opinions and experiences, you have a better chance of getting into a conversation.

"There are some key words that usually trigger reciprocity. Julie, if I were to call you today and say, 'Julie, you don't know me. I was referred to you by so and so, and I am working on a project in the insurance industry, of which I know little, and I need your advice,' would you meet with me?"

"Of course," I said.

"You see, too busy to meet does not even come into play. Bob, if I were to ask you your experiences about sales training, would you tell me about them?"

Bob replied, "Why, yes, of course."

"Patty," he asked, "if I were to show you a ten-week coaching plan and then ask you for your opinion about it, would you give it to me?"

"Sure, I would."

George said, "You mean you wouldn't say, 'I have to go run it by someone'?"

"No," Patty said.

"Of course, you would not, because I am asking for your opinion, not a decision. Salespeople ask for decisions way too soon, and they get put off. So early on, let's try to incorporate some questions that will help you find out what prospects know, their buying process, and how they feel about your idea, product, or service without insulting their intelligence.

"I would like you to take your qualifiers and see if you can incorporate one of these words in your questioning. The next words I will give you will help ensure that you open their ears early on. These words that invoke reciprocity are: 'advice,' 'help,' 'opinion,' 'experience,' 'belief,' 'importance,' 'priority,' and 'expect.'" He handed out some paper.

"Now, take a few minutes and create some questions that relate to your product and how you might qualify your prospect. Be sure to incorporate questions on the budget and decision-making process, too. Take some of those questions you asked earlier, and see if you can incorporate one of these words into those questions that you might already be asking. This is to improve upon what you have already learned. Work on them together, and I will be back in a few minutes." Here are the questions we compiled:

- From your past experience, how do you and your family make your financial decisions?

- From your experience, how does your company go about making these types of purchases?

- In your opinion, do you think your sales reps feel the need to get face-to-face with clients when making a service call?

- In your opinion, is it important to keep your employees finding new ways to reduce stress in their everyday lives?

- On a scale of one to ten, can you rate by order of priority these financial concerns?

- What do you believe is the biggest challenge in saving money?

- What do you believe is the biggest challenge in keeping employees motivated?

- I need your advice. We are considering taking our product to the training market, and we would like your opinion and input on how it might work in your industry.

- From your past experience, what do you budget for lunch-and-learn type of seminars?

- In your opinion, how much do you feel you and your partner would like to contribute toward your retirement accounts?

- How important is it for you to provide competitive benefits to retain your key employees?

- I need your help: Who do you know within your organization who might make decisions on lunch-and-learn seminars?

- In your opinion, is there anyone else in your organization who might be part of the process on a decision such as this?

- In your opinion, at what age do you expect to retire?

- Do you own any life insurance, and what has been your experience with insurance products?

- Have you had any experience with stress-reducing techniques at the workplace?

- What do you expect from a financial advisor?

A few minutes later, he returned and asked us to share our questions. He acknowledged that the questions were good, and I believe he could tell by the confidence in our voices that we were feeling good.

"Now," he said, "you might be challenged by the fact that you don't like their opinions, but you must never challenge what they believe to be true. For example, Bob, you may find that they believe your product is no different than what they can get for free on the Internet, or they already have a service with a big-name company. Julie, you may find they only believe in term insurance. In conversation and through the sales cycle, you must be careful not to challenge what they believe. I see salespeople challenging prospects' beliefs all the time, even the most experienced salespeople. For example, the prospect might say, 'I have term insurance. I believe in term and investing the difference.' Most sales reps are taught to show empathy by saying, 'I understand how you feel, many others have felt the same way.' What is the next thing out of the salesperson's mouth?"

Bob and I jumped in and said, "But."

"Yes, that is a fighting word. 'But I understand.' 'But my idea is better.' 'You look great today, but.' I love these management courses that teach how to give annual reviews. They tell you to make it balanced. First tell them the good, and then tell them the bad. In an annual performance review in 80 percent of America, employees hear, 'You're doing a good job in this area, here and there, but.'"

Patty responded, "The person forgets everything good you said."

I said, "I get defensive when that happens to me."

George continued, "Yes, 'but' and 'however' are fighting words." He handed out a little clicker and said for our next weeks together, anytime we used the word "but," we would click each other. "Let's get that out of our vocabulary to make sure when we are out there alone we are not fighting with our prospects. This is not our objection session, so let's move on to thought-provoking questions.

"There are only two reasons that people do not buy your idea, product, or service. Either they don't even realize they have a problem, or they are not bothered or provoked enough to do anything about it. Julie, most people know they will die someday, right? And most people know they will need insurance. Is that right?"

"Yes," I said.

"Then how often does your phone ring with people wanting to get insurance?"

"Just about never."

"That proves the point. Even when people know they need something, they may put it off because they are not aware of the pain that could occur if they don't get it now. Once more, too often salespeople jump into tell mode without creating an awareness or an interest based on the person's pain or problems.

"You must really put yourself in your customer's shoes for every encounter. This is why having a target market is important, because you can more easily identify the pain of a like group of potential customers. Then you can develop a few questions that will really make them think of or even feel their pain. How often has someone made a sales pitch to you, and your mind starts trailing off because you don't see how what the salesperson is saying has anything to do with you? How does someone sound to you when they are telling you what you need and you don't see the need?"

"*Blah, blah, blah,*" we said in unison.

"Now, a more challenging question is how often have you sounded like *blah, blah, blah* to your captive audience, your prospect? I want you to think of your ideal prospect, like we did a few sessions ago, when working on our phone scripts. We'll use it for part two of our questioning techniques. Go back and think of the problems and pain that could occur if they don't do business with you. Then try to put them in the form of thought-provoking questions or statements. If you jump into tell mode, then you could irritate the prospect. Have you ever had someone tell you what you need to do, because… ?"

We nodded our heads yes.

"How do you feel when someone tells you what you need or what you should do?"

"I think they sound like my parents," I said.

"Julie, did you always like what your parents told you to do?"

"No. As a matter of fact I rebelled much of the time."

"This is what your customers do, too. Let's help customers see their pain by using questions so that people will start asking you to solve their problems!

"These questions can be based on factual statistics that are startling, which means you might have to do a little homework. For today's purposes, if you think you know of something that would make for a startling statistic, use it and then do your homework to verify it. Always be sure you have a reliable and current source for your statistics, so it does not backfire on you later. It sounds more credible when you quote a statistic according to a reputable source.

"To help you shift from tell mode to ask mode, I'd like to do an exercise with you." George handed out a sheet with the following phrases listed and asked us to complete them in a way that would pique our prospect's interest.

- Are you aware…?

- Does it concern you…?

- Could there be a problem if…?

- What would happen if…?

- According to…?

- How would it feel if/to…?

- Did you know…?

- How often have you heard someone say…?

"Patty," he said, "let's use your Toastmasters speech to do a quick example to show you how quick and easy this is. Who is your target audience at Toastmasters?"

Patty answered, "There are usually about thirty people. We have everyone from the self-employed to several CEOs of companies."

"Patty, what pain do they have now, or could have, that you can solve with your products and services?"

"They have deadlines on presentations, employee downtime trying to learn software features, because they have not been trained."

George asked us to come up with several questions that Patty could use. He waited a few minutes, and then asked us to share. Here's what we came up with:

- "Have you ever worked on a proposal late at night that's due the next day and you couldn't figure out how to polish it?"

- "What could happen if you showed up at that meeting and your offer was great, but your proposal looked poor?"

- "Are you aware of the dollars lost due to employees' basic training skills being out of date?"

- "Do you ever wish you could find more time in a day?"

George continued, "If you have three questions like this, you are bound to hit on the pain of most of your audience. Your only goal here is to get them to open up and want to hear you. Just like you want a prospect to open up and hear you.

"The next thing you would do in your speech is to open up with a compelling message about what they will get or expect from your session. This message should be based on your solution or remedy, and remember—use your bridge. Think of the solution, the audience, and the purpose. Patty, go for it."

Patty said, "The purpose of our training is to make sure you are getting the most from your day, by getting the most from your people."

"Good. Now you will have to have some meat in your presentation to keep their attention, and we will get there in our next session. You will find that you can combine these techniques and use them to open up prospects in everyday conversations. For example, you can have a conversation with someone sitting next to you by combining a thought-provoking question, a reciprocity question, and a compelling message to generate an appointment.

"I am going to take it one step further. You all mentioned that your own networking group was struggling and is on hold indefinitely. Collectively, I want you to think of the problems and pain and challenges that other salespeople are facing and what value and solution coming to your group offers. We can use this later to promote the group as you begin your mentoring venture. Julie, you said you are involved in fund-raising for Community Treasure. I want you to apply this same technique to your efforts in fund-raising. Think about the prospect you are asking to donate money, and ask yourself, *What problems or pain will they experience if they don't contribute?* Turn it into some thought-provoking questions, and then create that message to open up their ears to listen to you and hear all of the benefits of being a donor. Come up with a list of how many people you know in your community who are out of work and struggling. 'Are you aware there are fifteen nonprofit organizations that benefit from the umbrella of Community Treasure? Do you ever wish you could contribute money where it's needed, when it's needed?'

"Before we part today, I would like your opinion on how you feel about what we have done so far together."

I replied, "Well, it has really turned my sales cycle inside out. It has caused me to think about my prospects' needs versus my product when I go out."

"What is the one most important thing you have learned to date?"

As Bob began to answer, I realized that George had been using the law of reciprocity since day one with each one of us… and Patty replied, "George, you have given me a confident approach that I've never experienced before."

Homework

Just as George gave us an assignment, here is your assignment to complete before you read the next chapter.

1. Create a flyer for each one of your businesses or markets using the technique from this chapter. Include reciprocity or thought-provoking types of questions, and then identify a clear, concise and compelling message about

what you do for them. Always remember: state your company, service, and product name at the end of your message.

2. Identify the problems and pain of those sales professionals who might be prospects for our networking group and the solutions and "pleasures we bring to them."

—CHAPTER SIX—

MAKING YOUR COMPELLING PRESENTATION

We don't argue with those who sell for less,
for they know what their product is worth.

—from the *Let the Customer Buy* selling course,
Lee Dubois

I arrived at 7:25 a.m. Everyone was already there, and I noticed the fervor and excitement in each of us even in the way we approached these sessions. As we reviewed our activity and results, it was incredible how all three of us had more prospects in the mill and already more work in progress.

Patty shared with us that another prospect bought a nine-day training session for his call center team.

Bob enthusiastically shared his numbers, noting his increase in activity. He also shared how the color-coding gave him balance of time. Because of the color-coding, he now has a routine in his day, something he said he never had before.

I was happy to share that I sold a business partnership protection agreement to a client I had wanted to work with for years. At the end of the transaction, I tried three in-your-opinion types of questions, which led to a proposal for the retirement plan for their business of ten employees.

Bob admitted that even though he is getting more appointments and he can see the activity is up, for some reason, people just aren't getting it. They are all saying, "Wow, this looks great," and downloading the free trial while he's with them. After that they just don't seem to use it. Bob explained his frustration with the fact that prospects seem excited during the demonstrations, but they don't use the service after that.

George focused on Bob, asking him to review and verify his numbers, which he did.

George continued, "You know this brings up a question, and the question is for all three of you. When you are demonstrating, are you selling from the buyer's perspective or yours?"

Bob answered for us. "Why, of course, we are demonstrating from the buyer's perspective."

"Obviously you have a reason for saying that, Bob. Do you mind if I ask you what it is?" George responded.

"I know that in my presentation, I tell them that we have the highest level of security because I know they are concerned about this. I tell them that we have no long-distance charges, and we have the best audio-video technology. Our security has features that meld with comprehensive WAN connectivity and routing."

George stopped him and said, "Bob, I want to clarify what you just said. You 'tell' them many things about your product, and you used the word 'tell' four times."

"Well, yes…"

"Bob, how do you know it is important to them?"

Bob didn't say anything.

"How do you know that security is important? Could it be that a person who is not familiar with your technology might not even know that this should be important?"

Bob replied, "Yes, I guess so."

George asked, "Julie, if we are so sure that people know insurance and retirement are important, then why is your telephone not ringing off the hook?"

We all sat there with dumb, puzzled looks on our faces. He had us. We were all selling based on what we believed should be important to our clients.

He didn't even have to say anything. It was as if the lightbulb had gone off for all three of us simultaneously. He continued, "Now, do you see the value of doing a good job with your questions? If you do not find out what their opinions and beliefs and concerns are, you are just telling them what should be important to them. In order to separate yourself from the competition, you must be able to match your feature or fact benefits to that particular person and specific situation. Your fact-finding will reveal specific buying motives. For each person, the logical reason for purchasing your product may be the same, but the motives may be different.

"Obviously, in your world, Julie, you need to make sure the presentation complies with insurance regulations.

"Let's look more closely at the presentation stage, where you convert key facts into benefits. As we discussed earlier, these are not benefits for the sake of benefits. The prospect must see them as benefits. This is pretty easy, as you have always been taught to follow a feature or a fact with a benefit, right?"

We all agreed.

He continued, "The question becomes, do you back up facts with facts or with benefits? What I want you to do is pick three or four key features of your product. We will now introduce the next bridge. Every time you state a fact or even some sort of claim about your product, you should follow up with transitional statements such as, 'which means to you,' 'in other words,' 'the real benefit to you is,' 'let me show you what I mean,' or 'the end result is.' This is how you create value statements.

"Bob, let's take you, for example. You keep talking about security, no long-distance charges, and real-time audio and video. Let's take each one of those statements, connecting one, two, or even three of the fact-benefit bridges."

George turned the page on the flip chart to a page with the heading:

> **FACT/FEATURE/CLAIM...BENEFIT...BENEFIT TO PROSPECT**

George continued, "Let's take those three tell statements you brought up earlier and try to fill in the blanks. Who is your prospect: the trainer, corporate exec, or sales rep?"

Bob said, "In this case, the sales rep. I'd start with, 'We have the highest level of security since we use INS technology in our firewall…'"

George interjected, "Which means to you…"

"'That hackers can't intercept your videoconferencing, and…'"

George filled in, "And the real benefit to you is…"

"'You don't have to worry about your customers' confidential information being revealed to the public,'" said Bob.

Bob continued on his own, "'We have real-time audio-video, which means to you that you don't have a distorted verbal or audio message as you communicate with your clients, and the real benefit to you is you'll feel like you are right there in front of them.'"

George said, "And the end result…"

Bob said, "'The end result is you can see more prospects and clients, waste less time, and put more dollars in your pocket.'"

"Good job," George commended.

Now George focused on me. "Julie, let's look at your sales. How often do people buy all those little benefits like the guaranteed insurability options or waiver of premium or even accidental death benefits on policies?"

"Never."

"Well," George continued, "is it because the benefits don't work for prospects or because you don't show the value?" George smiled and said, "Don't answer that, and let's give it a try. Start with the waiver of premium and try to wrap it using the short message technique. In other words, state the name of the feature toward the end of the brief message."

I said, "We offer a benefit that will pay your premiums on your policy after six months of a disability and it is retroactive..."

George coached, "Which means to you..."

"Which means to you that you will not have to worry about how you would be able to pay your premiums in the event of a disability, especially if you lose your job and cannot work."

George said, "And the real benefit to you..."

I replied, "Your policy, including cash values, is self-completing, which you can use for emergencies and opportunities or even retirement."

George turned his attention to Patty. "Patty, sell us as individuals on the value of attending one of your sessions or using the spreadsheet software."

Patty said, "This training will improve your technical and administrative computing skills, which means you will be more productive, and the real benefit to you is your team will have less errors, less stress, and less turnover."

We all applauded.

"Now," George asked, "in your opinion how does this compare with what you were doing before?"

I answered, "Wow, they sounded great! All of a sudden, I am realizing that Bob's product could help me stay in contact with clients who have moved away. All this time I have known him, I never really thought of his program as something I could use for my business."

George said, "That's great, and they did sound good. The key is not to assume that what you said sounds good to your prospects just because we thought it did. Would you agree?"

We all agreed.

Homework

1. Outline your key selling features

2. List your outstanding benefits and create a value statement.

3. Identify your add-on sales and identify features and create a value statement for each of them.

CHAPTER SEVEN

GETTING TO THE ASK

Are They Buyin' What You're Sayin'?

You can discover more about a man in an
hour of play than a year of conversation.

—Plato

George started in his usual chipper way. "Good
morning, and how are all of you today?"

Patty just jumped in, which was so unlike her.
She was bursting at the seams with a smile as big as
could be. She said, "Oh my gosh, things could not be
any better! I can't believe it. I did the speech at Toastmasters, and I used all of the techniques. I had three
people come up and ask me how they could get me
to do some training for their companies." Patty was
so impressed at how she really captured their interest.
Some of the VPs even stayed to ask her questions after-
ward. She also said that she sold six CDs, although

selling at Toastmasters was not her intent. She handed each of us one as a gift.

Bob said that he was doing really well, and he met with his marketing people to have them revise some of the flyers and brochures to reflect our new techniques.

George asked if they were offended, and Bob explained that they actually welcomed the suggestions.

George said, "OK, you seem to be creating a great deal of interest and excitement for your products and services. In this meeting we will discuss the difference between trial closing and asking for a decision, and more important, the significance of reading and interpreting verbal and nonverbal cues. The real benefit to you is that you will know where you stand in the sales process, and you will only ask for a decision when they are ready to buy. How do you know when your prospect is ready to buy?"

I said, "You know, George. You can just tell."

"How?" he asked.

"They just kind of lean forward."

Bob said, "Yes, they also say things like, 'Will it work on my computer?' or 'How much does it cost?'"

George asked, "Do you all feel you know body language pretty well?"

We all nodded.

"OK, then let me ask you, what does this mean?" He folded his arms tightly, clenched his jaws, and wrinkled his brow?

I said, "It means you are closed to my idea."

George asked, "Could it be that I am freezing?"

"Well, yes," I agreed. "I just sit with my arms crossed sometimes because it is comfortable."

George continued, "OK, what does this mean?" and he put his hand on his chin and moved his finger gently.

"It means you are interested or thinking about it," Bob said.

George continued, "Then what does this mean?" and he put his hand on his nose and gently rubbed his finger on his nose.

Patty said, "That also means you are thinking about it."

Bob said, "It means you have an itch," and we all laughed.

"It always amazes me that selling is all about communication and yet very few sales reps I meet know the true art of communication." He turned the page of the flip chart, and the header read, "Sources of Communication." A pie chart outlined 7 percent verbal, 38 percent nonverbal, and 55 percent body language.

"The good sales rep has learned to listen to the verbal buying signs such as order-asking questions, or even some of the basic body language, like sitting forward versus leaning back. Very few really study nonverbal communication, which makes up approximately 55 percent of communication. This communication can also give you hints when they ain't buying into what you are saying!

"First, you must be very careful not to ask for a decision unless you know the prospect is really ready to commit. What happens when you are shopping, interested in something—let's say a new mobile phone—and the salesperson tries to close you before you are really sold on the product or service. How does this make you feel, and what do you say or do?"

I said, "Sometimes I just shut down. As a matter of fact, that happened to me the other day when I was shopping. I was just looking at a piece of jewelry and the guy tried to close me. I ended saying thanks while walking away. And after I walked away, he kept jabbering."

George asked, "If you could have looked and thought about it a little more, is there a small chance you might have bought it?"

"Yes! It wasn't even that expensive. He just made me shut down."

George said, "The first thing we have to do before we ever go for a close or any type of decision is to really find out how someone feels about something. What technique did we learn that gets pretty sincere or candid answers?"

Patty said, "The reciprocity questions."

"That is right, Patty," George said. "So why not ask opinion-type questions at the close to get the person's opinion on the product or find out how it might compare to the prospect's experiences with our type of product?

"Julie, how would you have felt if the salesperson had asked, 'Have you seen this piece before? In your opinion does it compare well with what you have been looking at when you were shopping?'"

"He certainly would have gotten me into a conversation versus totally shutting me down."

"Yes," George said, "and more important, he could have taken your temperature to see where you were in the buying process. You might have told him his jewelry is the greatest thing since sliced bread, or you might have told him you saw the same one down the street for less money. Now he would have known what to say next. For example, he might need to build value to justify the cost. Maybe his product is hand-cut, a genuine versus synthetic gemstone. Too often the amateur who has never learned to sell value is just out trying to match price.

"Let's pick up where we left off. Let's assume that you know you did a good job. You put your cards on the table, you showed the prospect some facts and benefits. Instead of pushing for a decision by asking something like, 'Would you like it in red or green?' why not use the reciprocity questions and say something like, 'In your opinion, how do you like what we have talked about today?' Or every time you show them a benefit, you might ask, 'In your opinion, would this be of benefit to you in your situation, or does this program meet you expectations?'"

George asked Patty to share her message that we created in one of our earlier sessions. It was one that started off with "The purpose of this session today is."

Patty went back through her notes, and she read it aloud: one of her ergonomic approaches to sitting at a computer.

"The purpose of our session is to give you some tips for what you can do throughout the day to ensure your body stays aligned, giving you more energy, making you more productive and keeping you happy, and more importantly healthy, for years to come."

George said, "Now, you might believe that they believe this is important, so you might say something like, 'In your opinion, do you feel you and your company would benefit from having employees better trained on day-to-day computer skills?' Then you get their agreement. Another example could be, 'In your opinion, could your employees find and use more time from a day?' Or 'In your opinion, would you like your employees to be more efficient and in the long run save this company money, which would make you more competitive?'"

He continued, "First, you must remember, before you ever ask for a decision, you should invoke some reciprocity-type questions.

"Next, watch the body language. Does it imply that the prospect is buying or not buying into what you are saying? Let's look at some basics about body language."

George said, "There are countless cues, both verbal and nonverbal, that let us know if our customer is buying into our ideas, products, or services. For example, I watch for the position of the hands. In my experience, I've found that when someone's hand is on their chin, it usually means they are buying into what I am saying. Hand on nose usually means they are discounting. When they are tapping your materials with their hand or on the table, I have found that this usually means that they are buying into you."

I thought back to how often people tapped at the table and I ended up rushing through my next words, thinking I had a disinterested prospect. How many sales I must have lost!

George continued, "When you are ready to close and you ask prospects for their opinions or if you have met their expectations, you will usually see some hand and face gestures. The professional salesperson can sit back with confidence, evaluating and knowing without words being said what path he or she must take. Selling is like a game and games can be fun, so it might mean you have to show more benefits or some proof. If you went straight for a yes or no decision after your presentation, you could totally lose control of the sale and lose the game.

"So remember, when you start seeing the body language kick in, after you have delivered a benefit, use a trial close with a reciprocity question. For example, 'In your opinion, does this meet your expectations?'

In a perfect world they say yes! Here is the part where we may not like what they tell us. Maybe they will say, 'Gee, I really thought it would do more.'"

George encouraged us to do our own reading and research on body language. He proceeded, "After you state your value, prospects want proof. Remember, they need the logic. Be sure to provide examples, statistics, annual reports, analogies, or even a demonstration."

George continued, "At the time of the ask, it is important for you to have your backup information. It is also important for you to think in advance about any questions they may ask or objections they may have so you can be prepared. In a perfect world, you would take the prospect's temperature, and he or she would say, 'I love this. How do I get involved?' When this occurs, you know you did a great job in the sales process—specifically the interest phase.

George then stated, "One of the most overlooked steps to the sale is Step 4, the Conclusion. It's simple, but invariably overlooked. Help your prospect digest your presentation with a mini-message, reminding them of what they said they wanted and how your offering can do this for them. It goes like this, 'In summary, you said you wanted (fill in the blanks). This program will do this for you, it will...' and proceed to fill in the blanks of what the offering will do in a short, concise manner.

"More sales are lost because the sales rep simply did not ask! Step 5 is the Close. Let's look at some of the different ways to close or ask for the order. Remember, when you ask too soon, before you answered all their questions, that puts you into an objection battle." George then described some ways to simply ask for a decision:

- *Just ask.* 'May we get you signed up, or could we set up a lunch and learn for your employees?'

- *Give them some sort of instruction.* For example, Julie, you might say, 'I need you to take a physical.'

- *Give them a choice.* This choice close works great for phone calls. For example, 'In your line of work would morning or afternoon work best?' or 'Would Tuesday at [time] or Thursday at [time] work best for you?' Or you could show them option one, option two, or option three.

- *Assumed close.* You took the prospect's temperature, you received a verbal approval, so you just start writing up your application or paperwork.

- *Gift or inducement close.* Many firms offer a gift or extra inducement. Banks do it all the time to open new accounts. Bob, you might offer a free headset or camera or three months free. Julie, I don't think you can use this in your business as usually it is considered rebating.

"The main thing to remember," George continued, "is: Ask, then zip your lips. It may seem like the longest moment in your life. You will be tempted to talk, to keep selling. You must let the prospect come to his own conclusion or give you questions or objections as to why he doesn't want to move forward."

Homework

1. Look at your last fifteen formal presentations, and identify if and how you asked for the decision and its outcome.

2. List the objections from these fifteen meetings and other objections you experience.

3. Research on the Internet or buy a book on body language.

4. People watch. Go to a coffee shop, hotel lobby, or other public venue and match the communication to the body language.

CHAPTER EIGHT

WELCOMING OBJECTIONS

You cannot answer an objection, "but" you can answer a question.

—*Lee Dubois*

As usual, everyone arrived right on time. George started with a question. "What did you find to be your most common objections?"

Bob said, "I still get 'I am too busy and we already have it.'"

"What do you do when you get these objections?"

"Usually I thank the prospects for their time and I send a follow-up note."

"So you accept it and move on. Is this correct?"

"Yes, I guess so," Bob said.

George explained, "Remember, people object for two real reasons. Either they do not buy your idea, product, or service because they are not aware that they have a problem, or they don't feel enough pain to do anything about it.

"With objections the first one is rarely the real one. So if in fact you are answering the first one, you can get yourself into the land of lost sales very quickly.

"When you go shopping and the sales clerk says, 'May I help you?' how do you respond?"

We all said, "No thanks, I am just looking."

George said, "I can ask that question in every region of the country and every market and I get the same answer. We are conditioned to keep salespeople away from us. It always amazes me that retailers still teach their people to meet and greet with the same line that gets the same result.

"Too often, I see courses that state to show empathy, then address the concern. As a matter of fact, I was walking through a large call center one day, and they had the most common objections all scripted out. Right in the little book it said to show empathy, and had scripted, 'I can understand how you feel.' Guess what the very next word was?"

I said, "But."

George replied, "Exactly. It is like saying that the person's feelings or opinions are not important. 'But' is a fighting word. Managers do this all the time when giving feedback because someone told them to make it balanced. So they say, 'You're doing a good job here, but...' How does the employee feel?"

I said, "Well, it just discounted everything that was already said."

"Yes, and how open is that employee to the rest of the conversation?" George asked.

"Not open."

"How is that employee's attitude walking out of the room?"

"Probably bad."

"You are right. 'But' is a fighting word, and 'however' is no better." George replied, "Ah, where are your clickers? As you begin to integrate all these techniques, I want you to role play with each other and with the people you coach. Let's get 'but' out of your vocabulary. To me it is as bad as swearing while selling. Prospects can use it, and they own the right. It is your job not to get into the 'but' war. So I ask you to click each other when you hear the word 'but.' Very often we don't even hear ourselves using it. Replace it for now with the word 'and.'

"'I can understand how you feel, and....' Remember, the bridges that I taught you will keep you from saying the wrong thing most of the time.

"Certainly, I do believe in showing empathy if you really do know how they feel, so you might say, 'I understand how you feel. Others have said that.' Then be sure to say 'at first.' This phrase shows that others also objected, but later approved and changed their mind. Here is another thing: if you are working with an upset customer or a complaint, you don't say others have said that same thing; it makes it seem as though you are making this mistake with everyone.

"Here are the bridges for objections. I want you to memorize and use them in your personal life so that you are comfortable with them in your business life. None of us, including myself, is comfortable asking for a decision—even more so when we get objections. These bridges keep you calm, cool, and in control, without obvious control."

The guidelines that George gave us are as follows:

Objection Bridges

- After showing empathy, say, "Apparently you have some reason for saying that. Do you mind if I ask what it is?" It's a polite way of acknowledging concern and finding out what is really on the prospect's mind. The first objection is rarely the real one.

- Another bridge: "Just suppose that was not a concern. Then in your opinion, do you feel our product meets your needs?" The purpose of this bridge is to get the prospect back on track to the question you asked. The specific concern must be addressed. Here are some examples:

  1. If the prospect mentions price, the statement is: "Just suppose that price was not a concern. Then in your opinion do you feel our plan meets your needs?"

  2. If the prospect says his company already has a plan or a service: "Just suppose you did not have something similar. Then in your opinion do you feel our plan is a good one?"

George continued, "In other words, many times they will give you an answer to something you may have never asked them. In your case, Bob, with Mr. Hartwell, you asked him for an appointment and he was already telling you what he knew about your product by saying he already used it. You did not ask him what he knew. Or many times people tell you they are too busy when you did not even ask them if they were busy.

"This communication technique has been taught in sales for a very long time. This is the one most often misused and butchered. For example, you see many prospects bring up price, and then the sales rep says, 'Just suppose I could meet your price. Then would you do business with me today?' The salesperson uses it as a way to ask for a decision. If the prospect says yes, what position is the salesperson in?"

I answered, "The salesperson has to meet price."

George asked, "Now, who took control of the sale?"

Bob said, "The prospect did."

"Yes, and now what we see is many sales reps who beg and plead with their company to reduce price. If every company reduces prices, what happens next?"

I answered, "Quality goes down."

"Yes, and when quality goes down, a company becomes economically unstable or reduces costs, lays off people, or survives by using cheaper labor.

"This is why it is important to sell value and not price, and not to lay down on the first objection, which many times is price. You have to show the value of your product or service over your competition. Also, realize that many of these prospects today take negotiation, so they immediately try to get your price down. Or if they can't justify to upper management why they paid more, then they are forced to do business with the competition. People will pay more for value. They do it all day long, and you do it, too. Would you buy a computer that costs less money that is known to continually have problems?

"Let's take the two bridges and work with them.

"Bob, if a person says his company already uses videoconferencing, you can say, 'Many people we work with do, and just suppose for a moment that you had not been exposed to videoconferencing. Then, in your opinion, do you feel our product would be a solution for your firm?'

"Wait for the response. If the person comes back with 'no,' you might say, 'Now, obviously you have a reason for saying that. Do you mind if I ask what it is?' and then what?"

"Another objection," said Bob.

George asked, "What happened to 'We already use videoconferencing'?"

"Well, it is gone."

"That's right! Gone! Yet how many times do salespeople pursue that first objection as the real one? It's similar to the 'I'm just looking' of retail. And if you pursue it, then you usually end up chasing dead leads. So now, let's look at Mr. Hartwell's situation. Was the objection you answered his first one?"

Bob nodded.

"What are the odds he read and got excited about your very technical email and went to your website?"

Bob quietly said, "Probably slim to none."

"Yes, Bob, I don't want to hurt your feelings. You jumped in tell/sell mode when he had no interest, and you assumed your answer to why you're different than video would entice him.

"I would like for you to role play your most common objections. Don't worry about closing them or answering them. Let's just get used to these two techniques.

"Patty, you said yours was time. Employers are telling you they don't have time for training. Is this correct?"

She nodded.

"Julie, be her partner. Patty, you just went through your pitch, asked a trial close, and Julie says, 'Patty, this looks great, but...'"

I hit my clicker.

George responded, "Oh, no, Julie. The client can and will use 'but'! They own that right. If you use it back, you have entered into the 'but' war zone. OK, now go ahead, Julie. Give her the objection."

I started the role play with, "Patty, thanks for your time. This looks great, but we just don't have time to train our employees."

Patty said, "Just suppose for a moment that you did have time. Then in your opinion do you feel our training would benefit your employees?"

"Yes, it would be good, but I just don't see that it is worth the investment."

George said, "Patty, use your *obviously* bridge."

"Obviously you have some reason for saying that. Do you mind if I ask what it is?"

I replied, "No, I don't. We tried to implement this training before, and we could not get the managers to send their people."

"Here comes another bridge: 'That may be the very reason why you do implement this now, to show employees that you care, and the real benefit to you is that employees will have less stress and be better prepared for the challenges in front of them, and most importantly they will become a well-orchestrated team.'"

Now George turned his attention to me. I decided to work on Community Treasure objections. I said, "I can understand, Mr. Donor, how you feel. As a matter of fact, many others who contribute also contribute to other organizations. Donating with us will provide you with benefits for you and your family. You see, XYZ charity is a great cause and it supports one area, one problem, and certainly a valid problem, but..."

The group hit the clickers. I didn't know why.

Bob said, "Julie, you said, 'but.'"

"I did? I did not even hear myself."

"Try it again, because you were on the right track," George said.

"Well, you see, XYZ charity is a great cause and it supports one area, one problem, and certainly a valid problem, and that may be the very reason you might consider donating a few dollars to Community Treasure. Community Treasure is designed to support many organizations, including your charity, too. The real benefit to you is if anyone in your family is in need of a service, XYZ is open to you. For example, two of my friends were having trouble adopting, and they contacted Catholic Charities, a recipient of the program. The support provided to Catholic Charities by Community Treasure ultimately enabled my friends to be proud parents. Personally, I have a widowed aunt who has some trouble caring for herself. The senior program allows her to have someone come to the home three days per week. Without these services in our community, there would be more burdens on us, as individuals, to care for loved ones. In your opinion, do you feel it is worth it to donate something to Community Treasure, which supports a variety of charities, in addition to what you are giving now?"

"Good," said George. "Now, let's take a common objection for your insurance product. What's the most common objection that you get?"

"I want to shop around," I said.

George told me to say what I would say to a prospect, and that he would portray the prospect.

I said, "For a moment suppose there was no other company. If we were the only company, then, in your opinion, do you feel our plan is a good one?"

"Yes, but I never feel comfortable making a decision without sleeping on it."

George turned to the group, "OK, gang, where's 'shopping around'?"

Bob said, "Gone."

I continued, "Obviously you have reasons for saying that. Do you mind if I ask what they are?"

George answered, "We just believe that you should sleep on something and then, the next day if you are still excited, proceed."

"I can understand how you feel. Others have said the same thing, and I sometimes feel the same way, especially when it is an impulse purchase. Often people wait, then they get caught up in family things, and they say, 'We'll talk about it tomorrow, or sleep on it.' Then they come home the next day and someone is late from work, or the kids have a soccer game, and they had all good intentions and push the decision to the weekend. Then the kids' soccer tournament ends up taking all weekend. Before you know it, the decision is postponed indefinitely. I'd like to ask you: If you like what I have shown you, could you go forth and take the steps to get it going while you are thinking about it?"

George nodded.

I continued, "We will give you a physical at our expense. It takes about three weeks to process, and at that time we can answer any last questions you have or you can call me in the meantime."

"Great!" George said. "Now, let's discuss your sales association. You may want to sell someone on being on your board as you grow, correct?"

"Yes," we said.

George said, "OK, Bob, sell Julie on being on the board, except it is not really Julie. She is a member, and comes to all the meetings, but has not been really involved because the board meets at night and she does not like to work at night. She has her own business, and is well connected and full of fresh ideas. First call her on the phone and leave her a voicemail."

"Hi, Julie. This is Bob. When you get a chance, call me back about serving on the committee."

George exclaimed, "Bob! Come on now! After our past weeks, what did you learn? People are busy! There must be some value. Remember, in the voicemail, your only goal is to get them to call you back."

Bob tried again. "Hello, Julie, this is Bob. Give me a call, as I believe I have a win-win opportunity for both of us as it relates to the Professional Sales Association."

George congratulated Bob about referring to a win-win in the voicemail.

Bob and I continued the role play as though I had called him back. "Well, Julie, I called because we have a win-win situation. We have formed a committee, and we would be honored if you could serve."

"Bob, I would be honored, but I know your group meets at night, and as you know, I keep my evening business commitments limited."

"Just suppose that we had our meetings in the day. Then, in your opinion, do you feel it would work for you?"

"No, I am just so busy, it's hard to commit."

"I can understand how you feel. As a matter of fact, I am keeping my networking and serving focused as well. And that is the very reason we thought we would place you on the membership committee. We know you are professional and would not attack our members, yet you would get the visibility and exposure as our membership director. This means that your name and your company name go out on all correspondence to organizations in town. You can host the meet-and-greets for all new members. We thought for you, since you're self-employed, it would be like free advertising. Now we do meet at night only once a month, and we hope that you would find giving up two hours a month is worth it for the P.R. you will receive in return."

We all clapped for Bob.

George summed up our session. He ended by saying, "Practice, practice, practice."

Homework

1. Exaggerate these techniques as you communicate at home.

2. Take some extra clickers and give them to your family members. Have them click you anytime you say the word "but" or "however."

3. Identify the objection that is most difficult for you, and practice out loud using each technique discussed.

CHAPTER NINE

PULLING IT TOGETHER

Composers in the old days used to keep strictly to the base of the theme, as their real subject. Beethoven varies the melody, harmony, and rhythms so beautifully.

—*Johannes Brahms*

"So now," George said, "what I would like to do is spend some time reviewing everything we have worked on over the past few sessions, specifically the presentation stage of the sales cycle. Remember, selling is really just convincing people to your way of thinking, and it is not only isolated to product. It is related to ideas, too. As Bryan Dodge, a national speaker, says for those of you who have children: if you ain't selling them, someone else is.

"Let's take some facts and run them through the bridges to implement a trial close. Assume it is a perfect world and the prospect is in agreement. Then move into one of five ways to close the sale.

"Julie, when you sell the services of Community Treasure, are you calling on individual donors or companies?"

I replied, "I call on companies, and I try to get them to run campaigns for our charity for their employees."

"Now, tell us what problems or pain could occur if they don't run a campaign, and what pleasure or remedy the organization brings."

"Well, their employees may need our services one day, and it would make them feel good knowing that they supported us. If no one participated on a corporate level, many of the social programs would disappear. For example, there is one program that helps children prepare for the standardized tests they have to take for grade school. We also fund the Greater Senior Citizens group, and we are a huge sponsor. If companies don't help support us, we can't support them. Many of these people could be the employees' parents and grandparents. The pleasure is that now the employee would not have to worry if the parent needed special assistance, or rides to doctors, shopping, etc."

"OK, Julie, you are at an appointment with whomever you call on."

I said, "Either the CEO or the H.R. department."

"You are at an appointment with the H.R. department: Remember, let's tie it all together. You walk in and make conversation. You are in the presenting stage and telling them about one of the benefits of running a campaign. Let's role play. I will be the H.R. person."

I started the role play. "Well, George, as you know, we also sponsor the Greater Senior Citizen Program." George stopped me.

"Remember, say the name of the program last. Start again."

"One of the programs we sponsor ensures that our senior citizens who are in need of help get help. What this means is that those seniors in the community who may be in need of care, transportation, and even house cleaning can have access to it. And the real benefit to your workforce is that as many employees are facing the issues of caring for a parent, they will have outlets. The real benefit to your organization is that by participating, supporting, and making your employees aware of the program, you will have less absenteeism and less stress per employee."

George interrupted and said, "Show an example."

I pretended to pull out a brochure and said, "Let me show you what I mean. In the year 2017 alone, the service was able to provide X number of dollars in the form of services to those right here in our local community. Now the odds are, your employees, or a relative of your employees, was a recipient of some of these benefits."

George jumped in and said, "Now, trial close me."

"So, George, in your opinion, do you believe your employees would benefit from knowing their aging parents have alternate support?"

"Well, yes."

"Do you think it would even make them feel better when it's time to use the service, knowing they contributed?"

"Yes," George answered as he directed me to close the sale.

"George, that is one of the many programs we support, and what I would like to ask is if we might get the campaign started here this February. May we?"

"Yes," George answered.

I felt really good, and I think he could see it in my face. Bob and Patty sat there smiling as I was going through this process.

George continued, "Next, you will sell a very expensive pen that's new on the market, and the retail range is $150 to $3,500. You are to sell it to sales reps who sell to high-level executives. So go backward and think of the pain and problems that could occur if they don't have your pen, the pleasures and remedies that occur because they do own it, and then take it right from the beginning to the close.

"Patty, will you give it a try?"

She laughed and agreed to try it.

"Think problems pain / remedy solution. Bob will be your prospect. Start off with some thought-provoking questions to get him into conversation."

She took a moment and scribbled some notes, then told us she was ready to go.

"Bob, how important is it for you to wear a professional suit to a professional business meeting?" Patty asked. "Is it as important for you to carry and wear accessories that go with the suit?"

Bob nodded.

Patty continued, "The reason I asked is I noticed you are using a pen from a hotel, and we have a pen that is designed to reflect your image and send a message to your prospects."

Bob jumped in and asked, "What do you mean?"

We all just smiled as we realized, that's what was supposed to happen. I don't think Bob knew he was falling in the trap.

Patty continued, "This pen is professionally designed and most importantly is ergonomically fit to your hand, which means to you, while making a presentation, you will write neater and cleaner so your prospects get your message. The real benefit to you is that you don't have to worry about it smearing on your hands or more important your prospects' hands or shirt cuff."

George said, "Prove it."

Patty said, "Here, Bob, try it." Then as he was writing she said, "The retail dollar amount for our average pen for those spent by people in your field is $950. In your opinion, do you feel that is in line for something that adds to your presentation?"

I could hear George say "good" under his breath.

Bob said, "Well, it's a little high."

"How much would you like to spend?"

Bob said, "Wow, I guess I realize maybe I do need a new pen!"

George made some observations about the role play. "Bob, I could even see it in your body language.

Julie, did you notice when Bob moved in his seat and his hand went to his chin?"

"Yes. I thought he did it on purpose,"

"Well, Bob, did you do it on purpose?"

"No, I did not even know I did it," Bob answered. "Patty, did you see it?"

"No, I was too worried about what I was saying," Patty answered.

George continued, "Yes, and the better you are accustomed to the bridges, the more you can focus on what is going on around you. Now, I do believe Bob was really buying in, so I did not stop you when he objected. Patty, you recovered well. What I would like to do is get you focused on what happens when you don't get the perfect answer, so you can recover, avoid a fight with the prospect, and most importantly, avoid the price objection. The only objection he gave you was price, so before you reduce price, it's important to sell the value of your product.

"Let's do one more example and take it all the way through. Bob, let's get someone involved in your sales association. I had you do some homework about the problems, pain, and your remedy and solutions. Let's say you are visiting with someone on the airplane. They share they have been in sales for a while, and they reside in your part of town. Start with thought-provoking questions or startling statements, and walk it through. Julie, you're sitting next to him on the plane. Take a second, think it through, and remember, problems and pain, and the remedy or solution your group provides. Take a moment to think it through."

A few seconds later, Bob turned to me and said, "Gee, Julie, you're in sales. How often do you find yourself looking to share your good days and more importantly your bad days with other salespeople?"

"Often. I work out in the field, and some days I don't even get into the office."

"Do you ever find that when you go to some association or networking meetings it's hard to build friendships or share what's really going on in your life, because they fill the time with speakers and announcements?"

"Yes," I answered. "I go to a few now, and I enjoy some of the speakers, but you're right, it's hard to build friendships."

"Yeah, and at many of these meetings you would never share your bad day, because many are your prospects. Julie, the reason I'm asking you this is because I am part of a group that meets for the sole purpose of helping sales reps grow their businesses. We do this through coaching, sharing, and focusing on key issues relevant to us, including working on the basic communication skills that many sales reps tend to forget. Most of us have become friends, and we find that the leads are just a natural by-product."

George said, "Prove it!"

Bob continued, "For example, a few of us were at a plateau, so we worked together with a coach and now we use his tools for those in our group as sort of a self-tutoring, coaching environment. Even the best in sports have spring training and a coach. In your opinion, would you benefit from a group like this?"

"Yes," I said, "I probably would."

"Well," Bob continued, "we meet at 7:30 a.m. every other week at a local diner on Trinity Road. I would like to invite you as my guest next week. Can you make it?"

"Sure, sounds like a good group."

"Great job!" George said. Then he summarized what we learned. "You are really grasping the techniques. Remember, if you think about the problems or pain and go into ask mode before tell mode, you have a better chance of capturing prospects' attention. Once you have their attention, they are more likely to really hear what you are saying. Then, if you show them what it means to them and prove it, you have a better chance of closing them. If they can't see how it benefits them, you will get lame excuses, such as, 'I am too busy,' 'We already have something like this,' or 'We don't want to get involved now.'"

George gave us our assignment and reminded us that next week was our final session. We said our good-byes and tarried off to our own sales trenches.

Homework

George asked us to do one assignment. As always it's best if you do this homework before reading the next chapter.

1. Think about your wish list. In a perfect world, what would your world look like?

CHAPTER TEN

WINNING ATTITUDE

> You will be the same person in five years as you are today except for the people you meet and the books you read.
>
> —*Charles "Tremendous" Jones*

I dropped the kids off at school today and I thought, *I really have to commit to getting my formal designation.* I turned on my self-study audio book for my CFP designation. As I listened, I realized that all of my education—including my college degree, my insurance designations, and my licenses—meant nothing if I could not get in front of people to tell my story. As I thought this, I could hear the instructor in the background, on the audio recording, talking about pension planning and the tax implications, and some other *blah, blah, blah.* Not that insurance knowledge is unimportant; it's just that I had always been taught to stay current on my education and to use my driving time for learning. I am always driving around listening to audio books and podcasts on new insurance concepts and working on the next degree when, in fact, I never thought of doing the same thing to learn more about selling.

When I got to George's office, I shared my thoughts from my morning drive. I said, "I had a revelation in the car this morning as I listened to audio for my CFP designation. I realized that just because I am learning more doesn't mean I can sell more." I turned to George and said, "Look at us. We are all so enthusiastic and excited to be here. How can we keep that up?"

George noted, "That is a great point, and let's address your comments. Let's look at the good news, which is that you are getting results. And as we study the science of selling, even if a result is negative, that is sometimes good. Results are based on activity, and we can now look at your sales process and see what might be causing the result. All of you need to keep up your education. Stay abreast of your industry and products. If you don't, you'll be stale and not be able to keep up with the competition. I hope I have shown you how to take some of the technical jargon and put it in terms of the benefits to the client. Now, Julie, the question becomes how important is education over skill or attitude and enthusiasm. Would you agree?" We all nodded in agreement.

"I agree with the theory of making good use of the driving time, and it will be up to you to balance knowledge, skill, and attitude. While knowledge is power, it takes skill to communicate it and a great attitude to get up and love what you do, so that you will impact people daily. In other words, the brain needs healthy food, just like your body does. So first, all of you, I would encourage you to use your driving time for self-improvement. Carve time out for this each day. In order to do this, you must watch how you invest your free time. You know, I cannot tell you the last time I watched the local news. If something is important enough, it will find its way to me. You can get everything important that is going on in the world on the front page of a *Wall Street Journal*.

"Television can be a negative influence, too. There's nothing wrong with a good program now and then. Personally, I would rather be doing things that add to my success than watching hours on end of other people achieving their goals and dreams. I think about so many people who watch award programs like the Oscars, the Golden Globe Awards, or the Grammy Awards."

As George was talking, it was as if he had me pegged. I said, "I love that stuff."

"Wouldn't you much rather be using that time to plan and achieve your own goals?" George asked.

"I never really thought of it that way. It's a good point, George."

George continued, "In short, you must find ways to keep your bucket empty, so you are fresh for your clients. I suggest you listen to motivational audios and read motivational and communication books. I am a believer in the old classics, like *Think and Grow Rich*, by Napoleon Hill; *The Richest Man in Babylon*, by George Clason; or the *Psychology of Winning*, by Dennis Waitley.

"Remember, feed your mind as you would your brain, and work on your goals versus watching others achieve theirs."

George led us in a discussion about the details of financial goals. "For the most part, your financial goals are set by your lifestyle. I believe you should plan for all of your life. Do you know more people spend more time planning their holiday gift list or Thanksgiving dinner menu than they spend planning their goals?

"Not only should you look at your financial goals, you should set goals for all aspects of your life. Your final assignment will include working on your life goal plans.

"When we started our session today, we talked about the balance of product, sales skills, and attitude. I want you to balance your time by listening to motivational audios and music as well as listening to your product or education recordings. Get a journal and write down detailed specific goals for various areas of your life.

"Personal goals include what you want to do, your dreams that have been unmet, hobbies you wish to pursue, and what kind of parent you want to be.

"Education goals might include learning more about your work, studying a second language, or getting another degree. Something in this area could be as simple as reading a book a week.

"Physical goals include exercise, weight maintenance, a new physical activity like riding your bike, or a goal for riding a certain number of miles, or pushing your running distance.

"Spiritual goals could include goals for prayer, Scripture reading, reading faith-based books, meditating, or going to church.

"And finally, as I mentioned first, you need financial goals.

"Remember back to one of our first sessions, I talked about color coding? Orange reflects things or actions leading to long term results and this includes goal planning. I suggest you . I had you block out one day per quarter, to look at where you are as well as reevaluate your goals in all aspects of your life.

"You seem like you are all trusting and open. I see no reason that you can't share these goals, hold each other accountable, and help each other on life's journey.

"Your goals should be achievable and measurable; they should create a passion within you. Most of all, you should continually raise the bar, so you don't stagnate and go backward.

"Goals must be yours. If they are not, you may be working toward something without a purpose. For example, Julie, you might say, 'My goal is to make a company trip or be a member of the Million Dollar Round Table. You have to ask yourself why you want to achieve it. If you don't know why, maybe it is just an expectation someone else has set for you. There is nothing wrong with expectations; just don't confuse them with goals. Goals are not easy; these are driven by the passions within. You can find some motivational audios or even biographies to get you thinking on another level. Otherwise, you are only capable of being and earning what has been set for you by your own mental image.

"At the beginning of these sessions, we agreed that after the eight weeks, you would begin to mentor others. What have you done to promote your sales association you've started here? How are you going to carry out your plan of action?"

He was a little surprised when we pulled out our color flyer. We told him we distributed it last month to our email lists and we already have several people showing an interest. Here's what we showed him.

Are you looking for a quick easy way to make more sales???

THERE ISN'T ONE!!!

If you would like to improve production through practicing the tactical skills that keep more prospects interested, and shut the doors to the common objections, we invite you to participate in our ten-week Sales Study Group.

WHO: Sales professionals at all levels seeking to sharpen their skills.

WHEN: Tuesdays, 7:30 a.m. SHARP

WHERE: 800 N. Broadway, Suite 1400
COST: Pay It Forward

TO LEARN MORE, CALL:
Julie: 555-0123; Patty: 555-0124;
Bob: 555-0125

Epilogue

Three years later, our study group is still growing strong. We have members from every industry, and satellite groups outside our area have formed. We formalized our notes into a workbook for all new participants, and we have even created coaching guides. A national sales association contacted us after hearing about our success from one of its members and would like to implement the concept in the association on a national level. George would have been so proud of his pay-it-forward concept in the sales industry. Four months after our meeting with him, he was diagnosed with a brain tumor, and six months after that he left with his flags flying. His concepts and his reminders that selling is nothing more than good communication enabled many of us to be low-pressure, confident business builders who can deliver our message in a clear, captivating, and compelling manner. He is not here, yet his investment is!

About the Author

Mary Anne (Wihbey) Davis is the President and Founder of Peak Performance Solutions. She is an internationally recognized sales and management consultant and trainer, and has helped an international Blue Chip list of clients achieve bottom-line results with her dynamic leadership and expertise. Her articles have appeared in various publications, radio shows and blogs. Before founding Peak Performance Solutions, Davis spent 10 years as a successful sales professional with Allianz® Life of North America, consistently achieving Million Dollar Round Table results and winning performance awards. Her achievements led to her induction into the company's Hall of Fame, and she was the first woman ever selected to speak on the main platform at the Annual Leaders Convention. She moved from sales to the home office as Assistant Vice President of Professional Development.

Visit Mary Anne's website for more information: www.PeakPerformanceSolutions.com.

To contact Mary Anne, you can email her at: maryanne@ppstrainer.com.

Six Strategies to Increase Sales Activity Through Referrals

Tips from Mary Anne's sales and leadership blog at bit.ly/Peakblog

In life, there are three R's everyone has had to master at one point or another: Romance, Relatives and Roommates. As salespeople, you get the added task of a fourth R: Referrals. Referrals are an extremely powerful selling tool. Yet, why is it many people share in the difficulty of obtaining them?

Your best leads for new business and future sales are referrals that have been sent your way by a satisfied client, one who will attest to the value of your ideas, products and service. Maybe it is that you do not want to seem desperate or look like you are asking for a favor? Or, maybe you just do not know the right time to pop the question? There definitely are proven methods for getting referrals.

Below are six strategies to keep in mind as you are learning how to master the fourth 'R'.

1. **Connections** – every one of your clients, friends and business associates could potentially connect you with dozens of contacts. People prefer and are much more comfortable doing business with someone they know, or at least know of. When you have been endorsed by someone they know and trust, it is much easier to open the door. The possibilities for new connections are limitless.

Action:

You will not get referrals if you do not ask. Ask your satisfied customer for referrals. Take it to the next level, give them specific examples of companies or people that are your ideal prospect. I often have people send me their resume with a note to me. Make my life easy and help me imagine the person(s) to send it too. It's the same in any type of sales and service environment. Not sure how to transition from the end of a call to the referral? Use our "By the way" prospecting hook.

"By the way, as you may know, we find that our best source of new customers is satisfied customers like you. I'm wondering if you could introduce me to others in your (field, organization, circle, etc.) who would benefit from what we do and the service we provide.

2. **Social media** – different networking platforms like Facebook, Instagram, Twitter and LinkedIn are invaluable assets to your business. They are especially helpful when you are trying to generate referrals and acquire new clientele. If you have a name, ask your source if it would be okay to connect with the third party and use their name in the introduction. Know the purpose of each tool and be certain that your posts reflect your brand and image in the right way.

Action:

Identify your target prospects. Find out who knows who you want to know. Pick up the phone (yes, pick up the phone) and ask them for their help. I was heading down to a meeting in Houston with a Regional/Division Manager for a manufacturing plant we were already working with and I decided to look up my contact on LinkedIn (someone else was driving of course). I saw the prospect was connected to another client who was a Senior VP of another manufacturing company. I picked up the phone and he loaded me up with information about the prospect. Now we had something in common, including someone he truly respected and valued. Prior to that, I was just another vendor doing business out at one of the plants.

3. **Simply ask** – sales are often lost because a sales person did not ask for the order. It is the same with referrals. Do not be shy about asking for referrals. You are great at what you do and you add value to your clients' lives. Because of that, you should never shrink away from the chance to benefit someone else and enrich their experiences as well.

Action:

Ask for help. Back in my insurance days, I hit the wall. Well, a slump is a slump, but not when you have been asked to be the keynote speaker at the annual convention the following spring. As a matter of fact, the Event Planner was told to have a heart to heart with me, as it was October and I was nowhere near making what was needed to qualify for the convention, let alone be the "keynote speaker." I told her not to worry, and I would make my numbers, plus some. I picked up the phone to long term clients who I knew had a genuine interest in my success and used the powerful phrase, "I need your help" and proceeded to explain my dilemma.

Not only did the first contact give me referrals, he told me to stay on the line and proceeded to make a few three-way phone call introductions. Within two days, I lined up over 130 referrals. Not only did I qualify for the convention, this bold action and a year's worth of sales became the topic for my keynote.

4. **Help them help you** – when asking for referrals, describe the type of people or organizations that are your ideal prospects. If you make them think too hard, they will respond with the statement, "Let me think about it and get back to you." For example, if you are in job search mode, specify your target companies or the ideal role you are seeking. If you are looking for internal leads, ask if they can introduce you to people in that specific department.

Action

Prior to calling or asking for referrals, create a list of ten individuals, businesses or positions inside companies that person may have a contact. Reference it when asking for the referral.

5. **Offer incentives** – the type of incentives you offer should coincide with the type of business you run or product you offer. In addition to a free item, you could offer discounts, upgraded

packages, bonus material, or credit to their account. Do not be afraid to test various methods to find out what offer entices clients the most and encourages them to make referrals.

Action:

Banks do it, you can too. Obviously, you have to watch the business you are in, and stay not only within the realm of your company's guidelines but also your client's guidelines. Don't put them in an uncomfortable position, as it will backfire. If it's appropriate and makes good business sense, see what incentives you might offer. My financial planner is more than generous with sending me a $25 gift card to a nice restaurant.

6. **Reciprocity** – the law of reciprocity is if you give, you shall receive. If you see a need you cannot meet, make a referral. Remember, positive energy and good intentions always come back around. So look for every opportunity to promote someone and build them up. One of the most effective ways to elicit referrals is to give them bountifully yourself.

Action:

Give, give, give and don't worry about receiving. If you have ever worked with me, you know I get energy from giving. I try to give unselfishly, never looking for something in return. At times it seems to be the long road to referrals and business, but I believe it's the magic of reciprocity that has kept me in business for 24 years. It was not a marketing strategy. It's who I am and what I believe from my heart. It's a value I was raised with from the start. Inherently, I know that this simple principle works. Over the years I have stayed in touch with contacts, helping and giving for many years before, one day, they are in a position to give back. The funny part is that you may never get back from someone you gave to, but someone else's generosity will pour out on you. I promise you though, this is not one you can "fake until you make." Giving must become part of your DNA and when it does the rewards are endless.

Imagine your pipeline filled with so many leads you can't manage. Imagine your phone ringing versus you dialing. Imagine this wonderful world of selling is helping you make all your dreams come true. I believe selling is the greatest business in the world. If you are struggling or stressing about quota, then there is a good chance these tips are for you.

Good luck, God bless,

Mary Anne

THE SALES MESSENGER NOTES

THE SALES MESSENGER NOTES

_____

_____

_____

_____

_____

_____

_____

_____

_____

_____

_____

_____

_____

_____

_____

_____

_____

_____

_____

_____

_____

_____

_____

THE SALES MESSENGER NOTES

THE SALES MESSENGER NOTES